To Adrian, Charlotte
Ruby & Jonah

with love a very best wishes

John H.

# THIS IS 60 KING STREET

First edition 2022

ISBN 978-1-3999-1462-8

Published by The Regency Press

Typeset, printed and bound
by Beamreach Printing, www.beamreachuk.co.uk

## Acknowledgements

With heartfelt thanks to Wendy for her invaluable editorial assistance and to whom I dedicate this book.

It is most appropriate that tribute is paid to the photographic skills of Peter Spooner and, in particular, his work in resurrecting the near-half-century-old scrapbook.

We are extremely grateful to David Exley of Beamreach for his experience and advice in bringing this book to the table.

# THIS IS 60 KING STREET

*The century-long story of a majestic Italianate building*

John Howard

# Contents

# Introduction

No-one is better qualified than John Howard to relate the history of 60 King Street, Knutsford, an establishment better known from 1909 to 1973 as the Kings Coffee House, a period of 64 years when it was regarded as the cultural hub of the town and a genteel establishment serving light English food and beverages. In 1974 unforeseen circumstances dictated the need for it to change its modus operandi in order to survive. It became the La Belle Epoque in 1974, achieving a reputation for fine French food, until June 2019, when it was forced to close its doors after a bitter feud with its landlord regarding rental arrears.

John Howard's extensive involvement is due to his family's long connection with the property, one that dated back to the 1850s when his maternal great-great-grandfather, Tom Lee, purchased the site which included the Hat and Feather, a derelict inn, which his son Fred Lee (John's great-grandfather) developed and then managed, selling it in 1895 to Richard Harding Watt, an entrepreneurial local amateur architect, whose vision and desire was to build a memorial tower to honour the town's famous Victorian authoress, Elizabeth Gaskell, and with it a coffee house that would reflect her achievements and also establish a literary and artistically orientated catering business that would, he hoped, 'feed both the stomachs and the minds' of the local populace. Having succeeded in his mission, Watt was tragically killed in an accident, leaving his widow as sole owner.

Mary Ethel Watt then part-let one half of the building to the Knutsford Urban District Council for use as its offices, before gifting it to them in 1914. The KUDC vacated the building in the mid-1920s. Mrs Watt died in 1941 and with her ended the long-standing private agreements with her Coffee-House tenants, enabling the KUDC to take control of the whole property and allow them to let it to tenants as a business concern. The early death of an elderly first tenant led to Harry Howard, John's father, being offered the tenancy in the mid-1950s, thus producing a most unusual and coincidental situation in that Harry Howard had, in 1932, married Bessie Lee, whose grandfather Fred Lee was the former owner of the old Hat and Feather inn, which was where her father, another Tom Lee, was born. In essence, she was returning to the site of the former family home.

In 1965 John accepted his father's offer to sublet to him the recently vacated former music-cum-meeting room and this he converted into The Tavern, one of only three Danish restaurants in Great Britain. The serious illness of his father saw him succeeding to the head lease in 1969. This presented him with the opportunity to develop what was a genteel but stagnating business. This he did by attempting to recapture the artistic spirit and culture that Richard Watt had intended for his Coffee House in the early years of the twentieth century.

This meant introducing art exhibitions and opening a boutique gallery, selling exclusive and original giftware items. At the same time he refurbished the interiors, ensuring that the arts and crafts theme was observed and respected. Extra bedrooms were added and a small service bar, serving wines and spirits, built. It was a high-risk enterprise financed by turnover, which was brought to an abrupt halt at the end of 1973 by the government's introduction of the three-day working week, brought about by disruptive trade union action. This demanded a dramatic change of direction and, regretfully, after 64 years, the closure of the Kings Coffee House and the need for a partner with whom to open again, but now as the La Belle Epoque. The immediate and tragic death of his partner led to exhaustion and the need to exit the restaurant business. This was achieved by selling his share of the business and leaving the La Belle Epoque to flourish as a fine-dining French restaurant, which, sad to say, was ultimately destroyed through mismanagement by the then-tenant owners, leading to their eviction on a legal issue brought about by non-payment of rent to the Knutsford Town Council, leaving that body with a bill for a huge sum with which to make this beautiful and evocative building fit for the public to love and appreciate again.

# PREFACE

How could a zoom lecture on early London coffee houses trigger the birth of a book and be of some slight disappointment to its prospective author?

The knowledgeable lady giving the lecture had at one time lived in Knutsford but did not mention the fact that sometime in the recent past, until 1973 to be precise, Knutsford had its own very original coffee house and had done since 1909. Then, of course, this dunderhead realised that he had not taken into account the time factor and that for almost half a century, and since 1974, 60 King Street had been home to the La Belle Epoque restaurant and that it was almost certain that our excellent lecturer would have dined there, of course not knowing that she was dining in a former coffee house – and why should she? She would not know that a significant period in my career had been devoted to attempting to breathe life into what was the Kings Coffee House and to re-establish the values that architect-builder Richard Harding Watt had aspired to since the outset, that of a culturally driven coffee house, small hotel and modest dining establishment, and also to maintain the tradition of the first coffee houses in which people could meet and discuss the events of the day and enjoy local gossip. In the case of the Kings Coffee House such meetings could

also be between the wives of local industrialists and often between parliamentary wives residing in Knutsford's wooded suburbs and further afield.

That our charming speaker and possibly all who were following the lecture were unaware that the La Belle Epoque had succeeded to the lease of a property once occupied by a very stylish coffee house not only seemed an injustice but also showed that there was a serious gap both in the history of the building and, of course, in that of Knutsford itself. All this served to motivate me into sharing what I considered a grave omission and one very much in need of correcting.

Apart from being unaware of the presence of a coffee house, did people actually know who built 60 King Street? Who, indeed, had heard of Richard Harding Watt, an architect and builder who had introduced Italianate architecture to Knutsford thirty years before Clough Williams Ellis had built Portmeirion on the Welsh coast near Porthmadog and that his ultimate triumph had been his 1909 Elizabeth Gaskell Memorial Tower and adjoining Kings Coffee House? Who knew that the management of the latter was, of necessity, female, privately educated, well-bred, self-sufficient, artistically orientated, friends of his, be prepared to live on the premises without salary and run a business on a non-profit-making basis? (Any takers?) The very thought of this in today's terms would be deemed an insanity but Watt's ladies were very special people who shared his liberal-cum-socialist philosophy whole heartedly and who would soon welcome to their premises the likes of author John Galsworthy, suffragette leader Emmeline Pankhurst and C P Scott, the legendary 'Scott of the Guardian', as well as Knutsford's feminine elite and their town-dwelling friends.

A word, then, of the La Belle Epoque. It was easy for people to think that it had been a French fine-dining restaurant from the very beginning. After all, Richard Watt had designed and built his coffee house at the very time that the Parisians were enjoying this particular epoque in their history. The culturally savvy Watt had added various small appropriate additions to the interiors of what was basically a reflection of William Morris's Arts and Crafts movement. What was very obvious was that the interiors lent themselves beautifully to the essence of the Belle Epoque period and, after my departure, allowed the La Belle Epoque management to further embellish them. It was, indeed, a very beautiful French restaurant and later an equally glamorous wedding venue, all of which was so carelessly mismanaged over a period leading to it being sadly bankrupted in 2019.

I strongly believed that it was necessary to bring to attention this gap in the history of 60 King Street and its place in that of Knutsford's history. There was little alternative other than to go into print and to write a book that would hopefully be both interesting and entertaining and would illustrate events clearly and factually. I have found from experience that a historical book or memoir is best appreciated if it contains appropriate photographs or images within its pages. Momentarily I was stumped. Forty-five years on from 1973 and with a failing memory I had no recollection of anything that would suffice but then thought of a scrapbook that lay at the bottom of a wardrobe in my cottage. What I found was what I thought was treasure trove. You may differ.

I had never been a collector of anything other than when, as a boy, I collected stamps and army badges. What then had made me almost systematically retain the invitations to the musical evenings, I do not know, nor the other items relating to the regular musical programmes and the La Belle Epoque publicity material and so on. Neither do I remember photographs of the Kings Coffee House's original interiors. I must have a natural need to have one foot in the past. Perhaps I am a nostalgia freak. However, all would serve as a reminder of the four wonderful years 1974-1977 when La Belle Epoque ventured into the world of musical entertainment. The promotion and execution of it was to be my responsibility. The programme involved the presentation of, on an alternate monthly basis, chamber and choral music provided by Nick Smith's hugely talented musicians from the Royal Northern College of Music and jazz-related music by nationally known groups which emanated from Ronnie Scott's London agency, which ultimately led to many of the finest international artists of that period appearing. After this our very fortunate clientele were treated to a splendid five-course French dinner.

To return to the scrapbook, of which there was much that was not presentable, there was a sufficient amount that was, and enough to spawn a book. My album was, therefore, hacked to pieces, this to allow my energetic Yorkshire-born photographer Peter Spooner to work his magic and bring some very difficult items to photograph to a high-enough standard for inclusion. There were a lot of excited discussions regarding quality, selection and batting order. The result is as you see it. It is the best that could be done to produce a book that will inform Knutsfordians and visitors alike that before the advent of the La Belle Epoque, there was a cultured establishment serving fine coffee, known as the Kings Coffee House (1909 – 1973). The speaker whom I mentioned at the beginning of this preface might also be persuaded, with good humour, to include the story in her talks on the subject of coffee houses, be they in London or Knutsford.

# The Lees

To avoid misunderstanding, it is necessary to know that the picturesque Italianate building at 60 King Street, dominating Knutsford's main street, was built in 1907/8 for two reasons: the tall needle tower to commemorate the Victorian authoress Elizabeth Gaskell's association with the town and the major part of the building to be a coffee house and boutique hotel. The latter was named the Kings Coffee House due to its location in King Street. The stone column at the entrance, on which the names of England's kings and queens are carved, emphasises the fact. The Kings Coffee House traded elegantly until 1974, when its fragile economy was shattered by the introduction of Ted Heath's three-day working week, forcing it to close its doors. Not too long afterwards it re-opened, then as a French Restaurant colourfully named the La Belle Epoque, well chosen as the building was of that period and easily reflected that time of gaiety and frivolity emanating from Paris. It was the owner's intent to create a business that reflected France's reputation for fine cuisine. A short time after opening a programme of musical events was introduced that further enhanced La Belle Epoque's reputation for being a 'go to' place to dine and be well entertained. It traded variously, sometimes precariously and ultimately successfully, for 46 years before it dramatically and amid considerable controversy closed its doors, or, more to the point, had its doors closed for it. The apparently successful business that the La Belle Epoque was had long been at loggerheads with its landlord, the Knutsford Town Council, over the matter of non-payment of rent. The issue was resolved on a matter of legality and the tenants were forced to vacate. They apparently did so with little grace; the beautiful interiors were trashed and, at the time of writing (2021-2) this lovely building lies empty awaiting a new tenant who would be responsible for its restoration, with work estimated to run to many hundred thousands of pounds. He or she will need deep pockets.

It is much more pleasurable to return to the above reference to the Kings Coffee House or KCH, its origins, its 64-year-long history and the characters who were involved in its creation and management. The story commences in 1850 with the arrival in Knutsford of Thomas (Tom) Lee, an ambitious and successful Stockport licensee. Tom had been visiting his uncle Joseph Lee, a blacksmith/farrier, since childhood. Over the years he had become well acquainted with Knutsford, sufficiently enough to court and then marry Margaret Norbury, daughter of the widowed licensee of the Foresters Arms, a tavern in the Old Market

By the time of his marriage in 1851 the then 33-year-old Tom Lee had become conversant with Knutsford in every sense, particularly from the commercial aspect, and with his financial powder kept dry he sought an opportunity to invest his capital. That opportunity soon presented itself. Mid-Victorian Knutsford was a far cry from its bustling 18th-century Georgian heyday. The railway was nigh, the coaching trade much reduced, industry was gone, the last of the small mills closed and many of the town's numerous inns closed with them. Knutsford was becoming a prim Victorian country town; much of it behind the lower, eastern side of King Street was a maze of domestic and industrial slums. Tom Lee's keen eye was attracted to two ancient adjoining coaching inns, both derelict, namely the Hat and Feather and the Rose and Crown. The latter still flourishes today. Fifty years later the Hat and Feather would prove to be the site of the Kings Coffee House. Much was to happen before that happy event, however. The two inns at the time were occupied by sundry labourers, many of them Irish, most of whom were employed in the construction of the railway. They were paying little or no rent but Tom was in no position to develop the situation, having invested all his capital in their acquisition. Very shrewdly and with considerable foresight he had invested in property on the main street of a town which he knew would prosper in the not-too-distant future. He was acutely aware that both the inns extended to the higher street, Princess

**Tom Lee.** *The ambitious and far-sighted Stockport licensee who came to Knutsford in 1851 and bought the dilapidated Hat and Feather and adjoining Rose and Crown inns*

Place, later to be demolished in the early 1950s along with a row of similarly handsome Georgian buildings. Selling his Stockport business, Tom moved into the Foresters Arms and became the licensee.

*The old **Rose and Crown** and **Hat and Feather** inns purchased by Tom Lee. The latter inn, situated in the centre of King Street, was to become the site of the Kings Coffee House*

Street, and included stables, barns, piggeries and various outbuildings, one of which was an 'ale and porter' off-licence business which faced onto Princess Street. This he was later to develop into a wine and spirit merchant's premises and it would become the main source of the Lee-family wealth.

Gradually over the following years Tom was able to develop the two inns but not yet activate the necessary licences. Happily, Tom and Margaret managed to produce a family of four boys – Robert, John, George and Fred, in that order. Fred, the youngest, was to be my maternal great grandfather and would play a principal role in the story of the future Kings Coffee House. Tom then took family planning to a higher plane in that he made a will that would ensure that all his young men, when they, having achieved their seniority, would each be willed a slice of the emerging Lee-property cake. Robert, as the future head of the family, would continue to develop the Princess Street wine and spirit business; John was willed several lowly cottages and two small shops that Tom had secured in his original purchase of the two inns; George was willed the Rose and Crown.

***Fred Lee.** The licensee of the Hat and Feather, who sold the inn to Richard Harding Watt circa 1895, thus allowing him to demolish it and build the Kings Coffee House and Gaskell Memorial Tower*

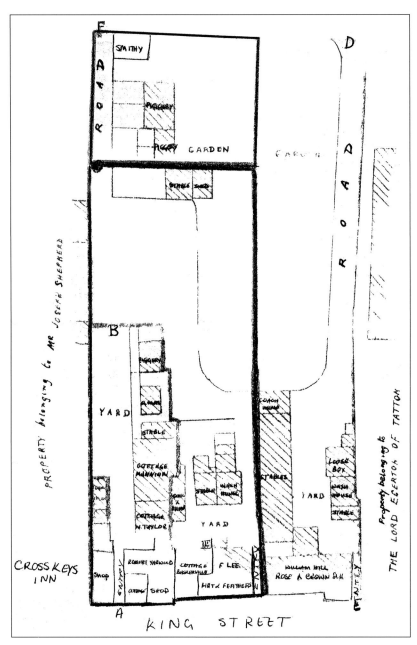

***The 19th-century plan of the Hat and Feather.*** *The rear of the inn extended upwards to Princess Street, Knutsford's other main thoroughfare. Not shown are the barns, stables, hen coops, piggery and smithy. The town's inns were more than self-sufficient.*

All would prosper. However, it is with my great grandfather Fred Lee that the storyline continues, this with his ownership of the Hat and Feather.

Fred was to meet and marry the girl next door, by name Jeannette Livingstone Jones, a Welsh girl from Holt, just over the county border with Wales. She was in service at the adjoining inn, the Cross Keys. During their time at the Hat and Feather they produced two boys, another Tom who was to be my grandfather and Oliver, my future great uncle. The inn prospered, a horse-and-carriage hire business contributing significantly to its overall well-being. The erection of a row of eight terraced cottages on his land at the rear of the inn and given to his wife as a wedding present was further evidence of a healthy financial situation. The sale or renting of the eight cottages in Church View, as it was known, brought further prosperity, the family retaining one of them for their own use. Fred's obvious wealth increased his status in the eyes of the town and led to an interest in local politics, resulting in his election, along with that of his older brother Robert, to the Knutsford Urban District Council. All was going swimmingly and would go increasingly so when a certain Richard Harding Watt arrived at his door and offered to buy the whole block of his King Street properties which included shops, cottages and, most significantly, the Hat and Feather. It was an offer that Fred Lee could hardly refuse.

# RICHARD HARDING WATT
# AND THE KINGS COFFEE HOUSE

***Richard Watt in profile.*** *The amateur architect and glove manufacturer who was to introduce an Italianate style of architecture to Knutsford. The ultimate example of this was the Elizabeth Gaskell Memorial Tower and Kings Coffee House of 1909.*

Who was Richard Harding Watt? In short, he was a man of huge talent and imagination with a vision and the will to impose on Knutsford, an ancient, historic and picturesque Cheshire market town, a style of architecture totally at odds with the attractive blend of 17th, 18th and 19th-century buildings that had made it so!

Not a lot is known of Richard Harding Watt's early boyhood except that in his later youth he showed a passionate interest in architecture and drawing. Little or nothing is known of his parents except that they were extremely wealthy, sufficiently so to enable him as a much more mature youth to undertake his own version of the 'grand tour' of the world, during which he was able to sketch many of the buildings which were of particular interest to him. In Brisbane, Australia, he tellingly worked briefly in a surveyor's office. On his return to England he studied briefly at the Slade School of Art and by his mid-twenties he had qualified as a teacher of drawing. All of this would serve him well in his future ventures.

The death of his parents meant that he succeeded to the family fortune as such. Whether his father was ever in the glove-making industry is not known. Richard Watt, however, was seen as the manufacturer of fine leather gloves with a head office on Piccadilly in Manchester and further offices in London and Glasgow. By an amazing coincidence it happened that his general manager and leather buyer was my grandfather Albert Howard, who accompanied him on his leather-buying trips to Florence in Italy. During this time Watt took the opportunity to sketch the architectural features of Tuscany's fine and ancient buildings. It would soon be seen that his endeavour in this direction would serve his future purpose.

We now find Watt living in Bowdon, then a village in whose leafy lanes dwelt Manchester's commercial and artistic elite – cotton barons, insurance and banking magnates, artists and musicians. Among the last group was Hans Richter, the famed conductor of Manchester's highly regarded Hallé Orchestra. However, it is with many of the wives, sisters and daughters of Bowdon's commercial and social hierarchy that Watt had an interest. There were a sufficient number of extremely talented female painters for them to be regarded as a colony. These ladies were the beating heart of a village with a culture-loving populace, being largely instrumental in the formation of dinner clubs and various societies. Watt was well conversant with this scene and was a good friend to many of the artists.

In 1895 Watt left Bowdon and took up residence in Knutsford. What his plans were at this juncture

is not clear. When they were eventually revealed, Knutsfordians were in for a considerable shock. He purchased a plot of land on the western side of Legh Road and built The Croft, a house in the Arts and Crafts style, a style associated with William Morris, the founder of that movement. Watt exhibited a drawing of the house in the Royal Academy in 1895, which was published in The Builder in 1896. By now it was becoming clear in which direction Watt was going after 30 years of fine-glove manufacturing. He was now ready to invest in his lifelong love of architecture but it was not going to be that simple. The early years of travelling the world and the many journeys he made to Italy and Tuscany to buy fine leather had made a lasting impression on him. If he was going to build, it was going to be in the Italianate style and this is an ancient and historic Cheshire town whose antiquated streets oozed a character enhanced by the former presence of the noted Victorian authoress Elizabeth Gaskell. Knutsford, quite obviously, for an architect who wanted to showcase his skills, was ideal. Anyone passing through Knutsford by train would be bewitched by the sight of its undulatingly compact antiquity. For an emerging architect of Watt's ilk and ambition it had the one great and necessary ingredient – it was built on a hillside, which would provide the more artistic architect the opportunity to achieve maximum effect. However, these were early days and Watt was not yet prepared to show his full hand. It was a case of softly softly. He was a long way off building the Kings Coffee House – twelve years to be precise.

To succeed in his ambition, Watt needed a little good fortune. That came in 1898 when he was able to buy John Long's tannery, situated as it was on the northern edge of the town. Here was shortly to be seen the first evidence of his attempt to give Knutsford another architectural dimension. He built a large steam laundry, not just a basic laundry but one that reflected his journeys in the Middle East. Now the northern edge of the town would sport an astonishingly harmonious array of buildings with a four-sided tower topped with an eight-sided pinnacle, which was a replica of one he had sketched in Damascus. The laundry chimney was enclosed in a minaret he had seen in Palestine. The domes of the boiler house suggested mosques and there were many features that reflected the architecture of the Middle East. He built a row of delightful balconied cottages along the adjoining Drury Lane for the employees. At the top of Drury Lane were added the Ruskin Recreation Rooms for the laundry workers. Watt strongly believed in the social function of architecture, not just as a means of improving living conditions but also for influencing minds. The Ruskin Rooms included a library and recreation room, along with reading, discussion and musical evenings. These principles to a great extent were to be incorporated in the future Kings Coffee House. The recreation rooms were intended to be available for public hire. Famously they were used as a meeting place for

***Watt's sketch for his proposed model steam laundry.*** *The Middle-Eastern extravaganza would alter the Knutsford skyline dramatically.*

***The finished laundry 1902***

the active branch of the local suffrage movement and many years later, in 1943/44, the American officers of General George Patton's 2nd Armoured Division used the rooms as their mess prior to their departure to the war in Normandy.

Richard Watt's intention to influence the architectural shape of Knutsford now took on an even more ambitious form. This time it was the southern edge of the town to which his attention turned and that was in his own back yard, so to speak. He purchased from the railway company what was considered to be a virtually unviable and quite useless stretch of land that extended along the western edge of Legh Road. That unviability was emphasised by the manner in which the land plunged quite severely into a valley at the bottom of which was the source of Knutsford's gentle little stream, the Lilybrook, the densely foliaged slope ending in a swamp. This did not deter Watt from his mission. The fact of the matter was that this hillside wilderness was precisely what he required to grandstand a project he had had in mind for some time. Now, that early period of his life spent travelling and sketching the world, and in particular Italy, was to bear fruition. He was going to build a row of Italianate villas that would eventually be the subject of much discussion, criticism and controversy. Love them or hate them, as Knutsfordians initially did, they have become the desired residences of Cheshire's wealthiest citizens. Viewed from the west of the town, Watt had created a sublime and exotic landscape, more appropriate to a Florentine suburb and one which he had known the wild hillside-site would provide him with.

To achieve the fame or notoriety, if you must, of these now-celebrated villas, Watt engaged the services of several architects, all of whom were going to have to adapt to his novel and often impractical ideas, as would the builders themselves, who would have to tolerate his indecision and changes of plan, if there was such a thing. The impatient and intolerant Watt would ride his horse on site, hectoring and bullying a workforce that once included a foreman who threatened him with a gun. Is it any wonder that one firm of builders left after being made to put up and pull down a tower three times? The architects, however, had one defining advantage over the builders in that, during their employ, they were taken to Italy to see and sketch the various towers, chimneys, skylines and other details that he had in mind. The question of detail was hugely important to Watt and he had his own daringly original approach to the matter. Wherever it was possible during his visits to Italy and indeed in other parts of Europe, he kept an eye open for architectural salvage and bric-a-brac including ironwork, stonework and fountains, all of which would be shipped home.

Much nearer to home he was equally industrious in acquiring much larger items that would more than suit his purpose. Most strikingly important were the monumental items of stonework that were piling up around Manchester as it underwent its transition from Georgian to Victorian. Happily for him, he could see from the window of his Piccadilly office the demolition of the Georgian Manchester Royal Infirmary, which would provide him with a treasure trove of pediments, architraves,

*The Georgian Manchester Royal Infirmary* as seen from Watt's Piccadilly office window

balusters and columns, not to mention gatehouses and small classical outbuildings. Moreover, when St Peter's Church was demolished, its huge columns were procured and taken to Knutsford in large wagons with six-foot high wheels pulled

*The remains of the MRI. All that was left of the MRI during the Victorianisation of the city. Much of the masonry ended up in Knutsford; Watt would find good use for it.*

by teams of draught horses. All this reclaimed material was then dumped on the various sites on which his villas were being built. Imagine the distress suffered by the residents of the mansions on the eastern side of Legh Road. Gone were their outstanding cross-country views.

This would be an appropriate moment to introduce Watt's architects and their achievements, taking into consideration the difficulties that presented themselves due to the idiosyncratic demands on their professional expertise. John Brooke from Bowdon was responsible for Watt's own Arts and Crafts home, The Croft (1898), and may have been involved with Moorgarth (1898) which was finished later by Harry S Fairhurst, who was taxed with the eccentric model steam laundry in Drury Lane (1899). Fairhurst was the first of his architects taken to Italy, to sketch towers and chimneys and to study the grouping of buildings in preparation for the Drury Lane project, a fall-out over chimney detail leading to his departure. He was followed by Walter Aston who was responsible for the first two of the 'famous eight' villas: White Howe in 1901 and Lake House in 1903. That same year Aston managed to squeeze in the Ruskin Rooms in Drury Lane and Cranford Gardens, the latter having a special place in the memory of the Howard family and one that will be elaborated on later in the narrative. 1904 marked the arrival of W Longworth who was to be responsible for the remaining six villas that adorned Legh Road: The Round House in 1904, High Morland and Broad Terraces in 1905, followed by Chantry Dane and Aldwarden Hill in 1906 and The Coach House in 1907.

This would suggest that Longworth was the main man in all this activity. He was certainly kept busy by Watt but according to 'well-informed sources' not in the most orthodox ways of the architectural profession. Watt was beginning to realise that his ideas might be better served if he took greater control of his projects and built them

**The Ruskin Rooms.** *Designed for the leisure moments of the staff of the laundry and a future general meeting place. In the 2nd World War it was the mess for the officers of General George Patton's American 2nd Armored Division.*

**Lake House.** *The Watt trademarks of towers, decorative chimneys, pantile roof, irregular window-spacing, random bricks and spaces for birds are all displayed. This 1902 house is different from the rest of the road-facing villas in that Watt built it facing south and along the slope of the hill leading down to Sanctuary Moor. Watt clearly enjoyed himself in building what is regarded as his masterpiece*

***Coronation Square.*** *Built in 1901 to celebrate the coronation of Edward VII, it fell into disrepair, was restored and 'bookends' the Knutsford skyline along with the Middle-Eastern laundry to the north.*

entirely himself with the minimum of assistance of an architect. He did not entirely dispense with the services of Longworth, retaining him for the duration of the time needed to complete the remaining half dozen villas, in a minor role as a draughtsman, model maker and foreman but not permitting any say from the design aspect. In an article on Watt in the Architectural Review of October 1940, by Aileen and William Tatton-Brown, it was suggested, and I quote, 'that Longworth was even made to sign a guarantee that he would only act as the architect's ghost, agreeing to the suppression of his name in connection with the buildings, so that Watt could retain the whole credit and responsibility himself'. I prefer to think that the future buyers of the properties would anyway be pleased to know that Watt himself had built their fairy-tale properties.

Watt, however, was far from finished in his endeavour to give Knutsford a slight tilt towards the Italianate. As related, in 1895 he had knocked on the door of Fred Lee's inn, the Hat and Feather, with his offer to buy it and the rest of the properties in the block that extended from the Cross Keys inn to the then Lee-owned Rose and Crown. Watt quite obviously had something grand in mind for what was, by his normal need for space to build, a very narrow and confined plot in an equally narrow King Street. There was also a significant fall in the land as it extended down the hill from Princess Street. Watt appears to have played a very canny hand, in that for a short period in the 1890s, as an elected councillor, he had chaired a committee of enquiry into the housing of the working classes which revealed that out of 584 houses inspected only 69 had water closets and 201 were without a proper water supply. He certainly would have paid particular attention to those in the block owned by the Lee family and equally to their market value when he made the offer to buy. Watt's hand had been stayed during the frantic period of the building of his Legh Road villas. That did not mean, however, that he had not given the King Street site his full attention

*Watt's 1905 sketch of his proposed Gaskell Memorial Tower and Coffee House*

from the planning perspective. He must have had a clear vision of what he wanted and now, after twelve years on the shelf, his plans were made clear and in 1907, after The Coach House had been completed, work began on what would become the Elizabeth Gaskell Memorial Tower with a coffee house and small hotel elegantly adjoining it - all, of course, in Watt's trademark Italianate style. The tall needle tower was dedicated to the highly regarded authoress who had resided in the town and written with great tenderness about Georgian life in Knutsford in the guise of her novel 'Cranford' and also in 'Wives and Daughters', the former being a particular favourite of Watt.

*The Elizabeth Gaskell Memorial Tower. Richard Watt's fine tribute to Elizabeth Gaskell, the revered Victorian authoress who resided in Knutsford as a child. Many of the characters in her books 'Cranford' and 'Wives and Daughters' were based on people in Knutsford with whom she was familiar in the late-Georgian and early-Victorian period.*

Elizabeth Gaskell was laid to rest in the quietness of the churchyard of Knutsford's unitarian chapel.

I referred above to Watt's 'trademark Italianate style', which was at the heart of his architecture. Yet, sometime much later another architect of note appeared on the horizon, also trading in the Italianate manner. This coincidence permits me to relate what I like to call my 'Portmeirion Story': Outside of Knutsford Richard Watt is little known. The more keenly interested in Watt's unique architecture are attracted by his Legh Road villas. What does surprise visitors is the sight of the Elizabeth Gaskell Memorial Tower and the adjoining building. A further short walk would reveal Watt's Middle-Eastern-orientated laundry and cottages, capped by the Ruskin Rooms. The more widely travelled visitor might be reminded of Portmeirion, the beautiful Italian-styled village located in Cardigan Bay in Mid Wales. The even better-informed traveller would have known that the visionary who built Portmeirion was a gentleman by the name of Sir Clough Williams-Ellis. He might even have thought that the Gaskell Memorial and adjoining restaurant owed their origins to Williams-Ellis. On the contrary, it could prove to be the other way round. This claim might upset Portmeirion admirers but spare me a few moments while I make my case, for which I make no apologies. Having related the following story in my book 'More Lees than Cheshire Fleas' and 'Tinker, Tailor, Soldier, Restaurateur', I have no hesitation in repeating the whole of it.

In the mid-1920s Clough Williams-Ellis was an aristocratic and autocratic wealthy landowning Welsh gentleman of considerable ancient pedigree who bought a coastal property named Aber lâ from his uncle Sir Osmond Williams of Castell Deudraeth. The property was located below Porthmadog on the Dwyryd estuary and overlooking Cardigan Bay. It was also just five miles from Williams-Ellis's own historic home, Plas Brondanw. The area of land comprised miniature cliffs, pinnacles, a plateau, a small valley, a waterfall and a coastline of rocky headlands, caves and small bays. This idyllic scenario presented Williams-Ellis, a practising and naturally gifted architect, though an unqualified one but, nevertheless, a fellow of the Royal Institute of British Architects, the opportunity to build an Italianate village. This was supposedly inspired by a chance visit to Portofino on the Ligurian coastline of the north-western Italian Riviera, Portofino's beauty being long acknowledged worldwide. Like Richard Watt, Williams-Ellis drew his architectural inspiration from visits to Italy, Watt, though, having made many more journeys there through his early youthful grand-touring and his later business trips; the latter were made some 30 or more years earlier. There was just one building on the newly acquired Welsh property. This was a large old house situated at the water's edge. In 1926 Williams-Ellis converted this into a hotel, not unlike, you may deduce, Watt's Kings Coffee House and Hotel of 1909. It was not as well conceived nor as well managed as the Coffee House, proving in its early days to be a somewhat disastrous venture until the intervention of James Wyllie, an artist and a former Oxford-hotel owner, who turned things around. From then on Williams-Ellis continued to develop the property, building his romantic and charming village, which was partially completed in 1931. You have read that Watt finished building the Coffee House in 1909: 22 years earlier! Williams-Ellis renamed his village Portmeirion and it could and would be said that it was now equally famous for its beauty as Portofino itself and deservedly so. It has subsequently brought great pleasure to countless thousands of entranced visitors.

In 1970 I had the privilege of obtaining the head lease of the Kings Coffee House, this on the death of my poorly father. Such was my pleasure in obtaining possession of a building dear to me as my and my family's home, a beautiful and famed building of Italianate design, that I was resolved to visit Portmeirion, feeling that I had something in common with that far more notable collection of Italian-styled buildings. Full of almost childish enthusiasm, I arrived there and almost immediately, to my utter surprise, saw walking towards me the legendary and easily identifiable figure of the great architect Clough Williams-Ellis himself – a beanpole of a man, then well into his eighties, very tall and gaunt and, as ever, clad in his almost-regulation garb of brown tweed Norfolk jacket, brown breeches, long yellow

**60 King Street.** *Late home to a bankrupt Belle Epoque restaurant and wedding venue. It still manages to look majestic.*

stockings, yellow waistcoat, bow tie and tweed hat set jauntily on his head. Unmissable!

I was almost overcome with awe at the sight of this imposing and celebrated figure, finding it hard not to genuflect due to my deeply held respect for the man. Nevertheless, I quickly resolved to speak to him as he advanced. I had little time to think what to say and what I eventually spluttered out was something along

the lines of "Mr Clough Williams-Ellis, forgive my impertinence in approaching you. What a marvellous place Portmeirion is! I live in an Italianate-style building in Knutsford built by a man called Richard Harding Watt". Without giving me time to say any more, he looked down at me (I am 5ft 10ins tall but was shrinking by the second) and, extremely coldly, said five short words. "I've never heard of him." was his reply and with that he brushed past me and was gone. I was left floundering like a fish out of water. I had deservedly been put in my place. At the time, the words 'I've never heard of him' meant little to me other than being a quick retort to dispense with my presence. I suppose he could have chatted for a few minutes to enquire exactly who Richard Watt was, but no, and I let the matter go. A few days later I began to recall my brief encounter and concluded that things did not quite add up. Here was a man of considerable knowledge and vast experience, sophisticated, well-read, well-connected and enormously well-travelled with a public-school education at Oundle, who had studied science at Cambridge and whose career as an architect took him the length and breadth of the country, including work at Bolesworth Castle for the Barbour family here in Cheshire, the castle not being that far from Knutsford. Portmeirion, anyway, is no more than 80 miles or so from the town as the crow flies. Chester lies just inside the Anglo-Welsh border and has been a trading destination for North Walians throughout the centuries. From there he would have taken the first-class railway journey to Manchester and could not have failed to be impressed by the panoramic view of Watt's Italianate Knutsford skyline, dominated to the north by the Middle-Eastern laundry and to the south by Coronation Square, with the Gaskell Tower and the Kings Coffee House proudly set in the centre of the town.

Clough Williams-Ellis, well-informed as he patently was, would as a practising architect have kept abreast of the latest information emanating from the architectural and building-trade journals. The 'Architectural Review' and 'The Builder' were must-haves for the working architect. He would also have read with keen interest Sir Nikolaus Pevsner's comments about Watt's Legh Road houses being 'the maddest sequence of villas in all England'. Williams-Ellis's interest in architecture would have made him aware that The Builder had published the drawing of Watt's first house and home, The Croft, a drawing which had been exhibited at the Royal Academy. What he would later read would be Marjorie Sykes's and Christopher Neve's four-page article in the Country Life magazine of March 1976, which heaped huge praise on Watt's endeavours, this being after my visit to Portmeirion.

It was certain that Williams-Ellis knew all about Richard Watt but why, on that day, summarily dismiss him? I came to the conclusion that I had pressed the wrong button and taken him completely by surprise, totally off guard, his five-word reply revealing hidden guilt. The man who liked to be called 'the father of fallen buildings' had suddenly been reminded of someone he knew had been collecting and collating architectural bric-a-brac and salvaged masonry and incorporating it into Italianate-style buildings in Knutsford nearly 30 years earlier. In fact, if Watt had been able to have had his way, Knutsford too might have looked like an Italian hillside town. His 1898 drawing of a proposed post-office illustrates this perfectly. He was also involved in the most impractical schemes for giving Knutsford a formal waterfront. We might have had earlier a vista akin to Williams-Ellis's Portofino.

My Portmeirion visit in 1970 and the consequent brush with Clough Williams-Ellis led me to take further interest in matters relating to this lovely Italianate resort. Courtesy of the Cheshire Records Office in Chester, I established through their company invoices and accounts that Caldwells of Knutsford had provided Portmeirion with a considerable number of trees, shrubs and bushes with which to adorn Williams-Ellis's project. Caldwells were perhaps the most highly regarded garden nurserymen in the north of England (they celebrated their bi-centenary in 1980). Williams-Ellis's visit to Knutsford to make his purchases would have taken him to Caldwells on the Chelford Road. It so happens that Chelford Road is a close neighbour to Legh Road, perhaps a hundred metres away, where Richard Harding

Watt's villas had stood in celebratory style for nigh on 30 years. I would think it quite likely that he took more than a peek at them that day and, equally, would have enjoyed lunch in Knutsford's most fashionable dining establishment, the Kings Coffee House. I cannot help but suggest that Portmeirion owed its origins not to a chance visit to Portofino but to Richard Harding Watt's Italianate adventure in Knutsford.

What, then, of the Kings Coffee House, as it was now known? Here we take a look back at the Richard Watt who built his Middle-Eastern style steam laundry and, in particular, at its Ruskin Recreation Rooms, ostensibly built primarily for the employees of the laundry but also for hire to the public. Watt was again to display his belief in the social function of architecture but on a grander scale. The Coffee House was to be no ordinary café or tea room; this was intended to effect both the atmosphere of a club and a Johnsonian coffee house. He was to create a cultural establishment that reflected his own liberal and intellectual views. He was going to influence and hopefully improve the human mind. To achieve this end, he introduced a first-floor smoking room in which there was a small library. Here the good citizens of the town could pop in during the day and evening to read the daily papers and magazines that were available, all without charge. This most beautiful room was used both as a musical concert room and as a meeting room. The room was to be the future home of a most original

and successful small restaurant. The interior decoration of the premises as a whole was stunningly of its day, being influenced by both William Morris's socialism and arts and crafts movement and by the art nouveau movement that was being showcased brilliantly by Charles Rennie Mackintosh, ironically via his Glasgow tea rooms of 1902. Contemporaneously Watt was introducing art nouveau features into his Legh Road villas in the early 1900s.

Who, one might wonder, would be able to manage such a high-minded establishment? This was not a business that required a hotshot manager. Sophistication was a prerequisite and it was essential that the incumbent should be a woman and preferably one with artistic leanings, who would reside on the premises and bring to the business the feminine overtone that a coffee house/tea room demanded. This would prove to be the case and the Kings Coffee House became quintessentially an elegant rendezvous for Knutsford and District ladies, who would easily identify with the management and their idealistic mindset. The Johnsonian coffee house atmosphere would soon prevail and with it the traditional amount of better-class gossip. The Kings Coffee House had little intention of obtaining a reputation for its cuisine; the food was to be simple fare. Its model bakery would bake its own bread, scones, biscuits and the like. The coffees and teas were, of course, the very finest.

*The frontal courtyard.* The door to the left was the
entrance to the first, 1907, phase of Watt's Kings Coffee
House. The second phase was completed after his purchase
of the former Hat and Feather inn from the author's great
grandfather, Fred Lee. The soon-to-be-demolished inn was
also where his grandfather, Tom Lee, was born. Carved
in stone above the window is evidence that these were the
offices of the Knutsford Urban District Council, who leased
part of the building from 1914.

*The covered courtyard. An extraordinary marriage of rural Italian domestic
architecture and neo-classicism with a glimpse of one of the two the Doric
columns that once graced the former St Peter's Church in St Peter's Square,
Manchester. Partially included in shot are the elaborate iron gates, the
Flemish lamp and the gift shop.*

Significantly, in accordance with Watt's liberal
ideals, the establishment was to be managed on
a non-profit-making basis. Ironically, not a lot of
profit could anyway ever be generated by such low
catering ambitions as were intended. This policy,
however, presented its own problems. It would have
to entail a high degree of competent management
and be a tightly run ship. Its overheads would be
enormous. This was a huge rambling building that
was heated by the modern central-heating system
that Watt had designed and built. Because of the
topographical features of the site the plumbing
system was diversity itself. The establishment also

needed a large staff of cooks, cleaners, waitresses, chambermaids and more. It was an organisational nightmare that would require the talents of very special people and not of professional ilk. Far from it! For Watt, the services of the talented amateur were a must and he had the answer, and had done, probably, since he purchased the town-centre site in the late 1890s. That answer lay seven miles away in Bowdon, where he had lived previously, as noted. We know that Bowdon was a cultural oasis, on the edge of industrial Manchester, in which resided a bevy of talented wealthy amateur artists, most of whom were the well-educated wives, sisters and daughters of Manchester's commercial and industrial elite, some of whom needed an opportunity to express themselves. Watt knew two of these, they being the Wilson sisters, Alice and Ethel. Both painted;

Ethel, in particular, was extremely talented and had exhibited variously at the Royal Birmingham Society of Arts, Manchester Academy of Fine Art, the Royal Academy of Arts, the Royal Cambrian Academy and more. The two ladies would create at the Kings Coffee House the artistic ambience that Watt required and that was happily in accord with his arts and crafts interiors. Soon the establishment was hosting painting and floral exhibitions and becoming the cultural heart of the town, with its largely female clientele comfortably at ease with the management, its femininity being further enhanced by the number of coming-out parties given for mid-Cheshire's young ladies. The ballroom, with French windows opening onto a large balcony and courtyard, provided a stunning backdrop and also served well as a gallery and exhibition room. Ethel Wilson was soon to marry

*The management and staff of the Kings Coffee House circa 1930.* In the centre is the august figure of owner/ manager Alice Wilson-Hall, who had managed the Kings Coffee House from the outset in 1909.

21

John Hall, a sub-editor at the highly regarded Manchester Guardian. They set up home at the Kings Coffee House to which his editor, C P Scott, the famed 'Scott of the Guardian', was often invited with his wife for weekends, during which they sketched and painted.

This is the moment to recall an earlier line in the narrative that referred to my grandfather, Albert Howard. By 1902 Watt's architectural plans were gathering pace. As a result, the glove-manufacturing business was becoming less important and appeared to be being 'put on the back boiler'; Watt seemed bored with it. However, it still had to be sustained. Watt had the answer. Howard and his family, plagued as they were by the gaseous airs of north Manchester's growing chemical industry, were transported to Knutsford and installed in the newly built Cranford Gardens. So Watt, with Howard his business manager and general factotum now only a stone's throw away from The Croft, was able to wholly indulge in his architectural adventures along Legh Road. Howard and Watt, it could be said, had enjoyed a good working relationship over the years, with the two men having travelled together on buying trips and enjoyed the social scene later in the day, with no shortage of female company. Then, in 1906, Watt married Mary Ethel

Armitage, daughter of a lift-manufacturing father with a factory in nearby Altrincham. According to Howard this was a tipping point in their relationship. To him Watt seemed a changed man, becoming irritable and difficult in their dealings. It is more than likely, though, that the two men had talked about the future and that Howard, after several years in Cranford Gardens, had intimated that his departure was imminent. He had, in fact, become the licensee of a public house, going in 1910 to the White Bear, the characterful 18th-century black and white timbered inn in Knutsford's Canute Place, where I was born. The fact that Watt retired in 1911 virtually confirms that the future had been discussed and decided by the two men.

**Cranford Gardens, Knutsford.** *Built by Watt in 1902 for Albert Howard and his sickly north-Manchester family*

***The Howard family in 1917.*** *Albert Howard was Richard Watt's leather buyer, general manager and 'fixer'. The small boy is Harry Howard, the eventual tenant and manager of the Kings Coffee House.*

Watt was now in a position to enjoy life in Knutsford. The Kings Coffee House was developing into the refined and cultured establishment that had been intended. The Miss Wilsons were succeeding in creating an atmosphere of enlightened gentility. The Kings Coffee House was the place to go, to meet friends and discuss life and events of the day.

For Watt the situation was ideal in a sense. He had his own gentleman's club in his own backyard. Here was the place to meet friends or fellow-businessmen. Although the Kings Coffee House was his last triumphant project, he was still architecturally active but in a less

majestic way, building cottages at the foot of Legh Road and restoring his earlier Coronation Square tower, built to celebrate the succession of Edward VII to the British throne in 1901. Watt also acquired a less-than-spectacular post office at the northern end of King Street and made alterations and there were a few out-of-town

***The bell push*** *grandly states 'to the garage', which was no more than an open space for two vehicles. However, in 1909 the horse and carriage trade still dominated in Knutsford; to accommodate two cars would have been a triumph indeed! The bell was more to alert the staff to the arrival of one of its more notable guests. The dark grey door is to the Giftique.*

commissions but nothing would ever match the splendour of his Legh Road villas. It was such restlessness that brought about his tragic end. Watt probably owned a car but on this occasion he chose to go down to Knutsford by horse and trap, standing upright like a would-be charioteer, as he often did, to enjoy the view of his villas, it is said, when his horse shied, throwing the 71-year-old Watt out of the carriage. He sustained injuries from which he shortly died. It would be appropriate and nice to think that it was Watt's intention to visit the coffee house, meet friends or talk coffee-house business with the Miss Wilsons. The year was 1913. Would this tragedy be a watershed moment in the short life of the Kings Coffee House? The Wilson sisters had assiduously applied themselves for the past five years to fulfil Watt's wish to create an enlightened establishment. With him now gone, what did the future hold? The Coffee House was certainly at the front of local politics. The women's suffrage movement was gaining momentum and the Kings Coffee House was hosting meetings of the Knutsford Division. It is thought that the Manchester-born leader of the movement, Emmeline Pankhurst, who had lived in Knutsford for some short time, would no doubt have attended. Certainly Watt's wife, Ethel, was an active member of the Knutsford Branch, attending the Kings Coffee House meetings. None, however, were more active than the Wilson sisters. Alice, in particular, was extremely so, achieving local fame for getting

*The recessed leaded **Oriel Window** beneath the Gaskell Tower is one of several such windows adorning the building. Few Knutsfordians would be aware of 'Tower Gate'.*

arrested and imprisoned for a week for throwing a brick through Bow Street police station's window.

It is with the widow of Richard Watt that we are now concerned. Mary Ethel Watt was now the owner of the Kings Coffee House. There were

**The Flemish Lamp.** *This fine photograph displays the charm and beauty of the ornate wrought-iron and stained-glass Flemish lamp that hangs, mostly unnoticed, under the courtyard roof. Watt is believed to have discovered it in Antwerp.*

no children to inherit Watt's fortune. She was elderly and would appear not conversant with the details of Watt's business dealings. How, one wonders, had she coped with the relationship

that had existed between her husband and the Wilson sisters? Were they to continue with the management of the business? With the departure of the newly-married Halls, John and Ethel, there was the arrival of Mildred Hall to assist. Doubtlessly she was a member of the Hall clan and probably John's sister. Happily she also was of artistic inclinations and her work was widely exhibited. Watt's tragic death unhappily happened at a time when the prospect of war in Europe loomed large. When the First World War did commence in 1914, it very shortly brought with it the casualty lists that would sadden the nation, and feminine conversation at the King's Coffee House would have revolved around the absence of their menfolk.

It must have been a confusing moment in Mary Ethel Watt's life when, not too long after her husband's death, she was approached by the Knutsford Urban District Council with a view to her leasing part of the very large coffee house to them. You do not need to be a scientist to figure out who was behind this approach. It is patently obvious that it was the brothers Robert and Fred Lee, both of whom were serving as Knutsford councillors at the time. Both knew Richard Watt very well and had served with him in council in the 1890s. It could be said that they both had an emotional attachment to the building, as it now occupied the site which their father, Tom Lee, had purchased circa 1850 and the site of the Hat and Feather Inn that Fred Lee had owned before he sold it to Watt. When Watt died, their interest in its future became personal and intense. Previously they had become aware that the Kings Coffee House had not been fully functioning in the manner that Watt had hoped and that the large first-floor music and meeting room was being barely used, if at all. So much, then, for improving the lives of the Knutsford menfolk, who quite patently preferred their public houses – and would not the inn-owning Lee family be delighted on that score? The KUDC was presently located in a dilapidated and ancient building further north along King Street that was shortly to be demolished.

With the assistance of Ethel's nephew, William Armitage, and a legal team she would consider the KUDC's approach, which was that she would be pleased to lease what could be said was the left-hand side of the building, if one was looking at it from the front. This would include the large first-floor music and meeting room, the ground-floor sitting room, six bedrooms and two bathrooms, all of which would be converted to meet the needs of the council. It should be noted that this would reduce bedroom accommodation by half. The remaining right-hand side of the building, including the coffee and dining rooms, kitchens, store room, ballroom, terrace garden and outhouses, sitting room and four bedrooms would stay with the owner. Then there was a huge change of mind by Mrs Watt, when in 1914 she

gifted the Kings Coffee House to the Knutsford Urban District Council, thus transferring the responsibility for maintenance and repairs to the council. Not included in the agreement were the buildings to the right-hand side of the property, mainly the coffee and dining rooms, the ballroom and the rest, which would remain in the hands of Mary Ethel Watt's estate and her tenants for 50 years. Up to 1933 the coffee-house side of the business was running on the same non-profit-making principles that Watt had insisted on. Then, on the 19th of May, the first tenancy agreement appertaining to the Kings Coffee House side of the business was agreed between Mrs Watt and her tenant, Mrs Jessica Wilson Hall – familiar names indeed. By the 1920s Knutsford was growing rapidly and with this growth the council's responsibilities. Departments were newly created or extended; additional staff were needed. In short, the premises had become too small for purpose. All of this necessitated a change of address and a move to the former prison governor's house on Toft Road was successfully negotiated. Mary Ethel Watt died in 1941 and, in 1943, her representative surrendered the ownership to the KUDC, which meant that from then onwards the tenancy of the Kings Coffee House would be tied to a rental agreement, which would be reviewed every three years. The Wilson Halls would now have to manage a non-profit-making business but, at least, they now had the whole building at their disposal to do so.

***Rear view of the Kings Coffee House.*** *A vista never seen until 2021 and courtesy of the Fletcher family.*

# THE HOWARDS

The Wilson Halls unfortunately were forced to surrender the lease due to the early death of Jessica Wilson Hall in the mid-sixties, leaving the KUDC without both tenant and manager capable of maintaining the style and necessary high standard that this elegant business demanded. Possibly, more to the point from the council's point of view, was the need to ensure that the position was filled as rapidly as possible. Delays could mean the loss of rental income. The Kings Coffee House needed to find a new tenant virtually immediately. The problem, of course, was finding a suitable candidate for the position. Preferably it should be someone local who had earned the respect of the town and its council. That person was to be my father, Harry Howard, formerly landlord of the White Bear and very much later of the Red Cow which was situated only 100 metres away across Canute Place. This hotel had been procured as a much more viable concern because of its number of letting bedrooms. Harry, however, not happy at the Red Cow, which belonged to Chesters Brewery, whose beers had a reputation for volatility and a chemical content that made them difficult to manage; their nickname was 'Chester's Fighting Ales', which was highly appropriate due to the fights that occurred at 10.30pm every Saturday

**Bessie and Harry Howard, 1950.** *Tenants of the Kings Coffee House from 1955 to 1970. Harry Howard was a draughtsman engineer who, when his father died suddenly, had unwillingly taken the licence of the White Bear inn, located in the town's main square. A keen sportsman, he was sufficiently well-regarded to be invited to take the lease of the Kings Coffee House. Bessie Howard's grandfather, Fred Lee, owned the old Hat and Feather prior to selling it to Richard Watt; her father, Tom Lee, was born there.*

***1909 interiors.*** *The interiors photographed in 1965 show little change from those of 1909. The whole of the ground floor, which included the Galsworthy Coffee Lounge and Gaskell Dining Room reflected William Morris's Arts and Crafts movement. The colour scheme was a subdued blend of soft organic greens and browns. The floor from the Entrance Hall and throughout the Coffee Lounge/Tea Room was a mosaic of small Venetian glass tiles, laid by Venetian craftsmen whom Watt had brought over from Venice for that purpose only. One dined off oak tables with inlaid marble tops. The seating was a mix of oak settles and settles upholstered in the adopted William Morris green. The chairs were oak with high backs and rush seating. The fireplaces were highly original; the one in the Galsworthy Room displayed a Viking theme. The Gaskell Dining Room was a delight; its two dining alcoves were always in demand. The one beneath the Gaskell Memorial Tower was through an arch supported by black marble columns. In both rooms a high shelf was backed occasionally by panels which favoured French country scenes. The shelves themselves displayed an eclectic collection of original ornaments that reflected the good taste of an enlightened earlier management.*

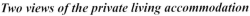

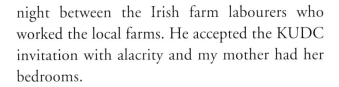

*Two views of the private living accommodation*

night between the Irish farm labourers who worked the local farms. He accepted the KUDC invitation with alacrity and my mother had her bedrooms.

The way of meeting the demands of a purchasing public was a far cry from what my father had been used to. He was something of a decent sportsman; as a youthful footballer, he had had trials with Grimsby Town, was on the books of Northwich Victoria and was a huge supporter of Manchester United. He was also a captain of Knutsford Cricket Club. His public-house life was a male-dominated one with conversation at the bar solely sport related; it included taking horse-racing bets,

collected by the local bookie's runner. Now he was behind a very different bar, one that sold cakes to mothers and chocolate to their small children, and he supervised an elderly all-female waiting-on staff. There were some lighter moments when local businessmen-friends came in for lunch or when L S Lowry came in, on most Saturday afternoons, for tea. For my mother the situation was a most unusual and very personal one. She was returning to the site of the former Hat and Feather inn, which her grandfather, Fred Lee, had sold to Richard Harding Watt to enable him to demolish it and build the Kings Coffee House. The former inn had also been where her father, Tom Lee, had been born. There were further

**THE KING'S COFFEE HOUSE**
**60 KING STREET, KNUTSFORD, CHESHIRE**
Tel.: 3060

### LUNCH 12-15 p.m. to 2 p.m.

**APPETISERS**

| | |
|---|---:|
| 1. Melon in Season | 17½p |
| 2. Soup of the Day with roll and butter | 11p |
| 3. Fruit Juices | 10p |
| 4. Liver Paté served with buttered Toast | 20p |
| 5. Prawn Cocktail | 25p |

**FROM THE GRILL**

| | |
|---|---:|
| 6. Grilled Rump Steak (8 oz. approximate uncooked weight) | 67½p |
| 7. Grilled Fillet Steak (8 oz. approximate uncooked weight) | 75p |
| 8. Grilled Pork Chops | 50p |
| 9. Grilled Lamb Cutlets | 45p |
| 10. Grilled Gammon Steaks with Pineapple | 45p |
| 11. Grilled Halibut with Tartare Sauce | 50p |

All the above dishes from the Grill are served with French Fried Potatoes and garnished with grilled Mushroom and Tomato.
or
any one of the following side salads:—

| | |
|---|---:|
| 12. Onion Rings in Anchovy Dressing | 12½p |
| 13. Tossed Mixed Salad with chopped hard boiled egg | 12½p |
| 14. Tomatoes stuffed with diced cucumber in mayonnaise | 12½p |

**SPECIALITY SALADS**

| | |
|---|---:|
| 15. Ham and Cottage Cheese Salad with Pineapple | 45p |
| 16. Cold Ham and Egg Pie with Salad | 35p |
| 17. Prawn and Apple Salad | 50p |

**LUNCH TIME SAVOURIES**

| | |
|---|---:|
| 18. Welsh Rarebit | 20p |
| 19. Buck Rarebit | 22p |
| 20. Poached Egg on Toast | 16p |

**SWEETS**

| | |
|---|---:|
| 21. Fresh Fruit Salad with Cream | 22½p |
| 22. The Cooked Sweet of the Day | 10p |
| 23. Fresh Fruit Basket according to Season. | |

**From our selection of Bertorelli Continental Ice Creams:—**

| | |
|---|---:|
| 24. Dietice | 15p |
| 25. Torrone | 17p |
| 26. Chocolat-Menthe Dairy Ice Cream | 17p |
| 27. Orange Surprise | 21p |
| 28. Mela Stregata | 24p |

A full description of these Ice Creams is on your table

**CHEESE**

| | |
|---|---:|
| 29. Brie. Rich and ripe from France | 15p |
| 30. Danish Blue | 15p |
| 31. Cheddar | 15p |
| 32. Cheshire | 15p |

Including Biscuits and Butter

**COFFEE**

| | |
|---|---:|
| Kenco Coffee, per cup | 6½p |
| Kenco Coffee, per pot, per person | 13p |

**MINIMUM CHARGE PER PERSON DURING LUNCH 30p**
**OUR TABLE LICENCE OPERATES UNTIL 2-30 p.m.**

coincidental connections. Her husband Harry, my father, was the son of Albert Howard, Richard Watt's former business manager and, it could be said, confidante and who was well versed in matters relating to the Coffee House.

It was at this moment that I hesitantly entered the picture. By 1965, at the time my father was accepting the lease agreement with the KUDC for the Kings Coffee House, I had married and was the father of my son, Clive, and was living in a quiet Knutsford backwater. A quick resumé of my working life means that after an undistinguished scholastic career and with my father determined that the hotel trade was not for me, I spent five years serving an apprenticeship in the tailoring trade in Manchester. This was followed by National Service, which lasted over two years, most of them spent with Sir Winston Churchill's old regiment, the 4th Queen's Own Hussars, which was stationed in Germany at

*The Kings Coffee House lunch menu in 1965*

Bergen-Belsen, that being the site of the former Nazi concentration camp. On demobilisation I was recommended to Harrod's Manchester store, Kendal Milne, where I did relatively well, obtaining a buyership in the men's tailoring department, buying men's leisure wear and ski wear. The job involved spending approximately two months of the year away, mostly in London but with flying trips to Northern Ireland to buy Irish linen jackets and to Scotland to buy Harris Tweed. The prize, though, was to go to Austria and affluent Kitzbuhel to buy the ski wear. It was a lotus-eating existence and we buyers were a pampered lot – and then the roof fell in.

*The Kings Coffee House afternoon tea menu in 1965. It is 50-plus years since food was offered at the above prices. It must be difficult for the reader to digest how ridiculously inexpensive dining out was then (see also the Tavern price list). How could Harry Howard take his profit? The time was approaching for change to take place at the Kings Coffee House. That time arrived in 1970 with the sad death of Harry Howard and the succession to the head lease of his son, John.*

## THE KING'S COFFEE HOUSE
### 60 KING STREET, KNUTSFORD, CHESHIRE
Tel.: 3060

### AFTERNOON AND SAVOURY HIGH TEAS 2-45 to 5-15 p.m.

#### SAVOURY TEAS

| | |
|---|---|
| Toasted Liver Sausage with Egg ... ... ... ... ... | 28p |
| Hawaiian Toast ... ... ... ... ... ... ... | 30p |
| Egg and Sardine Toast ... ... ... ... ... ... | 25p |
| Salmon Mornay ... ... ... ... ... ... ... | 28p |
| Welsh or Buck Rarebit ... ... ... ... ... 20p and | 22p |
| Devilled Sausages ... ... ... ... ... ... ... | 22p |

#### SPECIALITY SALADS

| | |
|---|---|
| Ham and Cottage Cheese Salad with Pineapple ... ... ... | 45p |
| Cold Ham and Egg Pie Salad ... ... ... ... ... | 35p |
| Prawn and Apple Salad ... ... ... ... ... ... | 50p |

From our selection of Bertorelli Continental Ice Creams:—

| | |
|---|---|
| Dietice ... ... ... ... ... ... ... ... | 15p |
| Torrone ... ... ... ... ... ... ... ... | 17p |
| Chocolate-Menthe Dairy Ice Cream ... ... ... ... | 17p |
| Orange Surprise ... ... ... ... ... ... ... | 21p |
| Mela Stregata ... ... ... ... ... ... ... | 24p |

A full description of these Ice Creams is on your table

#### SUNDRIES

| | |
|---|---|
| Buttered Scones ... ... ... ... ... ... ... | $4\frac{1}{2}$p |
| Toasted Crumpet ... ... ... ... ... ... ... | 5p |
| Toasted Teacakes ... ... ... ... ... ... ... | 5p |
| Fancy Cakes ... ... ... ... ... ... ... | 5p |
| Fresh Cream Cakes ... ... ... ... ... ... | $6\frac{1}{2}$p |
| Chocolate Biscuits ... ... ... ... ... ... | 3p |
| Plain Biscuits ... ... ... ... ... ... ... | $1\frac{1}{2}$p |
| Bread and Butter (Brown or White) ... ... ... ... | $3\frac{1}{2}$p |
| French Toast or Rye King (low caloried) with butter ... | 5p |

Sandwiches made to order from 15p.

#### BEVERAGES

The Beverages listed in the Morning Coffee Section are available throughout the afternoon.

# The Tavern

At this point I make no apology for turning to my autobiographical tome (Tinker, Tailor, Soldier, Restaurateur) for some of the narrative. The lotus-eating period in my life was very soon to come to an end. A dark cloud appeared on the distant horizon in the form of a rumoured takeover by the House of Fraser, the dreaded Glasgow drapers. If true, this meant rationalisation and the awful words 'central buying' were soon on every buyer's lips. The eventful sight of a brigade of severe-looking jocks in pinstriped suits and bowler hats marching in step through the store confirmed our worst fears. Our privileged little jaunts around the globe were soon to be a thing of the past. What to do? I was a member of a group of like-minded young men who were all good friends. Virtually to a man we were convinced that the future was indeed very bleak, and that it would be better if we sought employment elsewhere. Four of us did just that. However, of the four I was the only one who had not obtained a first-class job of work. I left with only a headful of half-baked ideas. Fortunately my wife had a good job of work as a secretary to the general manager of the then-new motorway service station on the M6 at Knutsford. We were dependent on her wages, that was until I could get some form of act together. My wage at the time of leaving the Harrods group was the princely sum of £1,000 per annum or £20 per week, a figure which everyone regarded as being the amount you needed to earn to be able to regard yourself as having 'arrived'.

Apart from the small sum withdrawn from the Harrods pension fund we had no other capital and yet I had aspirations towards owning my own business. I contemplated opening a sports shop: where and with what I do not know. I dithered and then obtained a lucky break. My father had by this time made his move from the eruptive Red Cow Hotel to the calm of the Kings Coffee House and was rightly being asked for a rent increase for that privilege by the owners, the Knutsford Urban District Council who, as has been stated, once used the building as the council offices after it had been gifted to them in 1914 by Mrs Watt. He had sublet the splendid first-floor concert and meeting room to the local De Tabley Masonic Lodge and was passing on to them a very small increase in rent, all quite normal. This was the sixties and the rent increase was proportionately low – a rate of £1 week, I think. My knowledge, however basic, of the Freemasonry movement is that it is made up of men who are not short of a 'bob or two'. However, this amount proved to be beyond their means, so they refused to pay the sum, packed their bags and moved to the vacant local electricity showroom.

My father then kindly offered the room to me at the same rent. I accepted, not yet having any idea what to do with it. After considerable deliberation and as the rest of the building was a catering establishment, I thought a food-orientated operation was appropriate. My wife and I decided to open a small restaurant and one which would not compromise my father's business downstairs, which would have been the unkindest of cuts. My wife, of course, was working for the Top Rank Hovis company who owned the Knutsford M6 service station; so she had one foot in the food industry.

I knew nothing but we did now have this empty superbly classy upstairs room with huge potential. What we needed was ease of operation – nothing as yet too ambitious, a small business in small premises, needing a small staff. Before leaving Harrods I had dined endlessly on cold-buffet food in the buyers' dining room and, with reservations, had enjoyed it. What could be easier than preparing food in one's own good time, placing it on a table for people to help themselves? Simple! A little too simple but hardly original. Practically everybody had eaten at some time from a buffet table. It is here that the old Harrods' training principles kicked in. Originality is the byword. How, then, to make something special and very different from the accepted cold-buffet format?

**The stone staircase** *leading to the former Danish restaurant 'The Tavern'. A large wooden cricket bat over the door indicated the restaurant's presence.*

Where did the best and most well-known cold food come from? Scandinavia, of course! – well known in Scandinavia but not presented in its true form to the British dining-out brigade. We decided to present food from Denmark in 'koldtbord' or cold-table style, along with Danish open sandwiches or 'smørrebrød'. I could at the time locate only two or three restaurants in Britain that served Danish food – the Old Howgate Inn, south of Edinburgh, a favourite of author William Boyd, and the Ebury Wine Bar in Ebury Street, London. Both, however, concentrated on smørrebrød. We visited both and found the field open for our enterprise but knew that a visit to Copenhagen might benefit us more.

Ideas are one thing; having the capital to finance them is another. Other than the relatively small pension sum in hand, we hadn't a brass farthing. We therefore wondered who might back us, if assured that in return we would back them by stocking their beers, spirits and wines. We decided to approach Bass Charrington, who duly and very kindly obliged. Their thinking may have been that, although we might never achieve a huge turnover, at least their goods would be on sale in a reputable little business in a characterful old Cheshire town and one in which their merchandise was

**The Spisekort (menu) cover**
*of the Danish restaurant, opened within the Kings Coffee House by John Howard in 1965. It was one of only three Danish restaurants in Great Britain and was Good Food Guide listed in 1966.*

# Forretter

# Danish Style Hot Dishes

**DANISH FARMHOUSE PÂTÉ**
Toast and butter     45p

**RENSEDE ANSJOVIS** Anchovies with
yolk of egg and chopped onion     50p

**Melon or Fresh Grapefruit**     25p

**FRUIT JUICES**     17p

**SUPPE** – We have two home made soups
each evening

**FORELLER** Smoked Trout     55p

**Corn on the Cob**     50p

**HORS-D'ŒUVRE FROM THE
COLD TABLE**     95p

**VINGJERGSNEGLE** Six snails in
melted garlic butter .     75p

**REJERCOCKTAIL** Shrimp Cocktail     45p

**POCHEREDE aeg** Poached eggs on
spinach masked with cheese sauce     60p

**RISTET FRANSKBRØD** Creamed
mushrooms and bacon on toast     45p

**BAEKFØREL**

Grilled Rainbow Trout, rubbed with garlic,
served with mushrooms, bacon, fried onions,
assorted vegetables, fried potatoes and
sauce bèarnaise     £1·40

**KALVEFILET MED SKINKE**

Escalope of Veal, served with ham & cheese,
asparagus, fried potatoes, and mushrooms
à la crème     £1·40

# Dansk Koldt Børd

– Danish Cold Table     £1·50

We strongly recommend you to our Cold Table. This offers a choice of some
thirty dishes, many of which have been specially imported from Denmark.
Start with a fish course, the sweet herring, smoked eel, followed by some meats
with rolled spiced pork, Danish salamis, green tomatoes in ginger, ginger pumpkins,
and the Danish salads. It is quite correct to make more than one visit to the
Cold Table.

**RØDSPAETTEFILET MIRABEAU**

Fillets of Plaice, served with spinach, asparagus
rolled in smoked salmon, peas, fried potatoes,
and sauce rémoulade     £1·50

**HALSTEGT MED RØDKAAL**

Fillet Steak, grilled and served with red cabbage,
assorted vegetables, fried potatoes and
mushrooms, with sauce bèarnaise     £1·60

# Desserter

Please choose your sweet from the dessert stand, or alternatively we have a
selection of ices, served plain or with melba sauce and nuts; fresh fruit salad,
or the fruit basket.

**LAMMEKOTELETTER CALCUTTA**

Lamb cutlets, grilled with pineapple, banana
and mushrooms, served on saffron rice with
creamed curry/sherry sauce     £1·35

# Cheeseboard

A selection of Danish cheese, together with Stilton and Cheshire Cheese,
is always available on our cheeseboard     20p

**COFFEE** Black or with cream     15p

**KYLLINGER MED LØG**

Casserole of halved baby chickens in cream
sauce, served with fried onions, bacon and
mushrooms on saffron rice     £1·35

***The menu detail*** *of the Danish food offered at The Tavern* not so well presented, which was precisely why we chose them. Anyway, the amount of cash we needed was 'peanuts' to them.

The room was gorgeous, with a rich panelled Japanese pitch-pine ceiling, huge windows and an entrance to the Elizabeth Gaskell memorial tower. There was also much evidence of Richard

**Danish Koldt Børd** – *the Danish cold table*

Watt's love of art nouveau, via door and window fittings in brass and copper that simply glowed. To function as a restaurant, we needed to fit a kitchen in a very small space, toilets and an equally small bar which would sit in the entrance to the tower, carpets and curtains, but most of all we needed furniture in the form of tables and chairs. The height of the room was such that at normal table-height we felt that people would be dwarfed and dominated by the extremely beautiful ceiling and that it might be better to raise the tables up a little, to enable the diners to appreciate it. We designed our own furniture and had it hand made locally. It consisted of long high tables with tall stools, the latter proving to be a challenge to older customers who might be prone to fall off them after a few drinks. There was also another particularly distinguishing feature; the table legs were specially made oversized cricket bats! Don't go away!

I decided that even with the natural charm of the room, it needed further added interest and, although I despise the 'themed' restaurant concept, the room still needed a story but one that was not at all gimmicky. I confess to being a cricket enthusiast – 'lunatic' might have been a more accurate description – in those days. I was extremely involved with the game at local level through my village team, Toft Cricket Club, being long-serving secretary, part-time skipper and coach to a large junior section. Hence the cricket-bat table legs, to which were added framed

*The Tavern dining room*

cricket-club ties and antique cricket prints. The menu was in the form of a large cricket ball and the wine list in the shape of a cricket bat, both, of course, in card form. It ended there and was done with subtlety. However, I had contrived to make the room look part restaurant and part cricket pavilion. The business needed a name and one that would easily spring to mind. I chose The Tavern – the fact that the public bar at Lord's

Cricket Ground is known as 'The Tavern' had nothing to do with it; I kid you, of course it did! The restaurant sign announcing this over the door was a huge wooden cricket bat.

So, there we have it, I suppose it could be said – a curious mix of Danish food, cricket theme, art nouveau interior, all in an Italianate building administered by two would-be restaurateurs. But it was to work splendidly. Another rather significant thing at the time was that I applied for and obtained, from a cricket-loving chairman of the local magistrates' bench, a licence to sell liquor. I was a licensee, the very thing that my father had not wished me to become, because he and his father, my grandfather, Albert, had either unwittingly or reluctantly entered a business to which they had an aversion and which had oft treated them unkindly. This was unlike my mother's side of the family, the licensing Lees, whose chosen profession it was, mayhem or no mayhem.

The Tavern was opened in May 1965 by Manchester's Danish consul, Mr Edward Bacon, or Danish Bacon, if you prefer, a most charming man and future good customer. My wife trained an honest, homely and capable female cook and administered to the kitchen in general. In true Harrods' tradition, with merchandise knowledge essential, I applied myself to learning the wine trade. My public-house upbringing had taught me enough about spirits and beer; the wine business was naturally a sheer joy to be involved with. I introduced myself to it through Raymond Postgate and his little red book, 'The Plain Man's Guide to Wine'; he became my mentor and was also responsible for the publication of every serious restaurant-frequenter's bible, 'The Good Food Guide', to which all aspiring restaurateurs endeavoured to be proficient enough to gain entry.

The emphasis in the 1960s was heavily weighted towards French and German wines. The Australian, New Zealand and Chilean wines had still to appear over the horizon. The business was all about Bordeaux, Burgundy, Loire, Alsace and Rhone wines from France and the Rheinhessan and Rheingau wines from Germany. We were aiming to attract an upmarket well-heeled and fairly enlightened clientele who would be likely to know their onions, or wines to be precise. I simply had to know at least as much about the subject as they did, preferably more. We were very soon to visit all the French wine-growing regions. It was easy to be enthusiastic and, if you are that, you are home and dry. I shall never understand restaurateurs who make no effort to learn about the wines they are buying and selling. They really should not be restaurateurs at all; good food should relate to good wine. The two go hand in hand. Instead, the less knowledgeable or ambitious leave it to the wine merchant. That could mean buying the wines he wants to sell for his own good reasons. Anyway, he would really prefer to talk to someone who appreciated his skill.

*The Tavern dining room with Tower bar and wine cellar*

When my wife left Top Rank Hovis, she brought with her waiting-on staff from the Knutsford M6 service station. They were mature ladies of the 'Hello, luv! What would you like?' variety. We dressed them in our chosen brown and beige uniforms and unleashed them, but on whom? I did not believe in advertising, so no-one knew we existed; we were not at street level and therefore had no shop frontage. We were upstairs and really needed some finding. Our cricket-bat sign was all that could be seen over the door at the top of a small staircase. I simply believed that, if you are good enough, you will do the business and that word of mouth was the way forward and the best form of advertising. The trick was to get the first customers up the staircase. We had two on Monday, the first night, and none then until the Saturday, when we had six. This was all too much for the waitresses, used to motorway bustle; they packed their bags and left. From then on we employed young housewives whom we knew mainly as friends and who were charming, with a young Danish girl to give credence to our venture. It all worked like a dream. After three months we were doing two sittings Saturday nights and were pretty full during the week, both at lunchtime and in the evenings. We had, however, to change our 'cold food only' format by adding a hot-food menu to our Danish 'koldtbord'; we just could not envisage our customers eating cold food on cold wet Cheshire winter nights. After six months we had earned an entry in Raymond Postgate's 'Good Food Guide'. Hallelujah!

Our clientele we got to know and on a fairly personal basis too. Being up front is essential in a small business and I was always to be seen. I simply had to handle all the wine and liquor orders as well as customers' bills. We had a big sporting following and naturally they were mostly cricketers, included amongst whom were the West Indian test team players, Clive Lloyd and Lance Gibbs, the England and Warwickshire fast bowler, Bob Willis, and other county players. We were also almost the unofficial headquarters of Cheshire County Cricket Club, who were dining with us on one occasion when news arrived that a good result in Devon meant that Cheshire were the minor counties champions. This was the beginning of a long relationship with the Cheshire club. Actors Richard Todd and George C Scott, the latter when playing the part of General Patton in the film 'Patton', were occasional diners, whereas Omar Sharif was with us on numerous occasions; a fervid bridge player, he had a regular rendezvous with a Mr Morley, a Knutsford man and frequent customer of the restaurant, who played to a similarly high standard.

# THE KINGS RESTAURANT

In 1968, after only three years' trading, we were going along at a great rate of knots, when two things occurred which changed the whole picture. My marriage got into difficulties and, even worse, our landlord, my kind and patient father, after several unsuccessful operations, was in a life-threatening condition and unable to conduct his own coffee house and hotel business, the Tavern, of course, being only part of the hotel and catering complex that the Coffee House was. The whole business needed to be made secure. My father needed to step down but my hard-working, volatile and vulnerable mother was not the person to take over the administrative responsibilities of the business. Both she and my father believed it to be in the best interests of all parties if it were possible for me to take on the head lease and, at the same time, the management of the hotel and coffee house; it seemed the obvious answer. Knutsford Urban District Council, via their excellent town clerk Edward Morley (not the bridge-player), instinctively knew that this was the best solution and so it came about. The business was made secure, my father could be nursed, my mother made safe and I was the sympathetic landlord to my wife and the Tavern. The year was 1969 and I now held a seven-year lease that, all things being equal, would need renegotiating in 1976.

My father by now was undergoing very serious operations, the final one being for a cancerous tumour of the brain. The portents were ominous. He was released from Salford Hospital and came home to be nursed by my mother in what was a busy and noisy environment. Poor father! It had been only ten years since he had finally left the licensing trade behind at the Red Cow Inn. He had not been there for that many years after spending a lifetime at the White Bear; the move just 100 metres across Canute Place had been induced by a better wage offer from Chesters Brewery, the owners of the Red Cow and by the fact that the inn had several guest bedrooms which would allow my mother to gain profit from their letting. Then came the offer from the Knutsford Council of the tenancy. It must have been a considerable jolt to my father's lifestyle to leave the masculine for the feminine. All his life had been spent in the smoky low-ceilinged rooms of a public house and he was, by the way, a heavy smoker himself. His customers were mainly men of varying social backgrounds, from the cheery grimy-faced workers at the nearby gas works to the city gentleman stopping for a quick drink on his way home after a day in his Manchester office.

# Things aren't quite what they used to be at the King's Coffee House

Preservationists and traditionalists however need not be alarmed. Nothing will ever be done to change the immense character of our beautiful late Victorian Dining Rooms. The atmosphere will remain heavy with the literary memories of Mrs. Gaskell's "Cranford" and John Galsworthy's "Forsyte Saga". The architectural dreams and design of Richard Harding Watt are safe in our keeping.

Indeed we will endeavour to highlight and feature the handsome Art Nouveau interiors and further the historical, artistic and literary themes. However we are not a museum and despite the many sophisticated talking points our business is people and good food.

During the luncheon period THE KING'S RESTAURANT is two restaurants in one.

**The Red Galsworthy Room is now a self-service cold buffet room, essentially English in its gastronomic offerings. Catering both for the hungry and weight conscious. A bar built by local craftsmen incorporating all Richard Watt's original styling has been added and is most complimentary to the cold buffet. The seating arrangements are also most original and again compliment both bar and buffet.**

**The Green Gaskell Room is now our Grill Room specialising, of course, in the grilling of steaks and other cuts of meat and fish. Gone is our "meat and two veg." image. We believe that we are now able to cater for the needs of the more sophisticated and discriminating diner. We may now be of particular interest to local businessmen and business organisations situated in the surrounding area, who, when entertaining colleagues and customers from home and abroad, might choose to enjoy both the food and the atmosphere in this uniquely Italian building. After all there is nowhere quite like "The Kings" in the whole country.**

By the way we are a small exclusive private Residential Hotel, RAC, AA appointed. Well reviewed in *Harpers & Queen* by Humphrey Lyttelton last February catering for the individual not wishing merely to be a room number.

Our final plans regarding our cuisine and our hours of business have not yet been determined but we do have a few more original ideas tucked up our sleeves.

## The King's Restaurant

60 King Street,
Knutsford.

*Tel: Knutsford 3060.*

CHESHIRE LIFE SEPTEMBER 1973

My father, the complete sporting man, would have to miss out on conversation concerning cricket, football and horse racing. No bookie's runner would be collecting bets from the Kings Coffee House. He would never hear a swear word again. Instead, he would be offering a selection of fancy pastries and cakes, to be boxed and taken home by young well-to-do housewives, whose clamouring children had been appeased by the selection of fine Swiss chocolate which was on offer at the counter. His largely feminine clientele would sit and chatter for hours on end over a cup of coffee or tea. His day would be briefly lit up at lunchtime when local businessmen popped in for an inexpensive lunch and a brief 'mannish' chat. Always a quiet man and a perfect gentleman, my father would have soon settled into his new way of life.

Pity, though, my poor father on his arrival at the Kings Coffee House! Gone were the glory days of this enlightened business venture; time had taken a deadly toll. Richard Watt had endeavoured to ensure that his project, opened in

***Things aren't quite what they used to be.***
*A declaration of good intent, Cheshire Life September 1973*

1909, harmonised with the thinking behind his building of the Elizabeth Gaskell memorial tower, which was the architectural cornerstone of the whole building. It had mattered greatly to Watt that the Coffee House should echo its literary and artistic connection with the town's great authoress. To achieve this, he had engaged the talented and artistically inclined Wilson sisters, Alice and Ethel, to whom I have referred in the chapter regarding Watt. Their success in achieving Watt's ambitions is, I hope, well noted. However, from 1909 to the mid-1960s is a long time to be running a business and maintaining high levels of excellence and intellectual integrity. The two bright young things in their early twenties and thirties in 1909 were now well advanced in age and in their late seventies and eighties. I know nothing of their demise or departure from the Coffee House; my father would certainly have known but I was not aware of the circumstances, being now married and busily engaged managing and buying for Harrods' Manchester store. Whatever the circumstances of their going, it is not hard to visualise the immediate problems facing him, after so many years. The familiarisation process alone would have

**The Kings Restaurant cover 1970**

47

taken months to absorb. Knowing my father as a thorough and painstakingly careful man, as befits a former draughtsman engineer, I also knew him to lack imagination in the business sense. He certainly was not the entrepreneurial type. However, for the first time in his life he was no longer a wage-earning public-house tenant with few opportunities to be expansive. He was finally in control of a business that offered him the chance of making capital gain and profit. He was his own man at last.

What, though, were the chances of making such profits? I have to say, in retrospect, that they were minimal. His relatively short stay at the Red Cow would not have allowed him sufficient time to accrue much capital from his hotel-bedroom-letting business. Above all, the run-down Kings Coffee House was in great need of capital injection and tender loving care, to restore it to its former glory. Certainly, he inherited a business that was up and running. Unfortunately, though, it was running out of both time and steam. It was being managed as well as it could possibly have been under the circumstances by a Mrs Jones. Again, I iterate, I had no knowledge of the whereabouts of the Miss Wilsons, although I feel sure that only Alice remained to the end as tenant and owner; Ethel, having married Manchester Guardian sub-editor, John Hall, had departed earlier. Vast amounts of money needed to be invested in the business to modernise and bring it back to the real world. It still echoed the Edwardian period

in which it was conceived. Father had not got the kind of money needed, so it became more of a holding operation – a gently-gently, see-how-you-go affair, with most attention being paid to the general cleaning and overhaul of the building. The Knutsford Council, of course, as the landlord, was responsible for maintaining the structural condition of the building but my father had to tend to the interiors which included the outdated kitchen equipment, most of which needed replacing. The much-vaunted model bakery, in which it had baked its own bread and confectionery, had long gone and was now part of the living accommodation.

As well as having to adapt to the existing way the business was being conducted, my father also had to give due consideration to the staff he was inheriting. These too, of course, were all ladies and, if not well-advanced in age, were mature, to say the least. There was an able cook, producing traditionally good but modest food, and there was an abundance of kitchen assistants variously employed with preparation and washing up. It was, though, the front-of-house staff that demanded father's total attention. This was a brigade of formidable, matronly middle-aged ladies with minds of their own who, dressed in black with white aprons and caps, went about their business of serving morning coffees, lunches and afternoon teas with great solemnity and dignity. My father had for some time had to exercise much patience with them; he was the new boy and they ruled their particular roost. If there appears to be an allusion to hens, then it is entirely accidental. He eventually got on extremely well with them; after all, he had been serving beer to most of their husbands in past years.

Such was the scenario into which I too, with trepidation, entered. At the time I had little heart or enthusiasm for it; it was a step back in time. I had virtually inherited the same problems that my father had had on his arrival. There had been little investment – more restoration and replacement than progressive modernisation. He had just not had the money for it. Now I too was in the same position. After just three years of opening the Tavern and making it into a popular and successful restaurant, I had left it without either rancour or profit. It was unthinkable that I should ever demand capital from it; I left it without a brass farthing to show for my endeavours and with nothing to invest in the Coffee House itself. I was starting from scratch all over again but, at least, it was a business that was up and running. At first, I was a little too reluctant to get involved, perhaps feeling a little hard done by. It was, after all, a far cry from my beloved Tavern, full as it had been with excitement and with its lively throng of interesting people to keep me on my toes. I was to lose my sporting and cricketing associations. No longer would I be buying and serving fine wines; the Coffee House was 'dry' and unlicensed. I would have

to settle for serving coffee and tea instead. I had to grit my teeth and get on with it for everyone's sake.

Gradually I grew to love the old place for what it was and I became absorbed in its history and background. I came to understand much better the spirit in which it had been conceived, so much so that I resolved to endeavour to resurrect, however slowly, some of the things that the King's Coffee House had been famous for, other than serving home-made patisserie. Along with that, some modernisation had to take place, such as would not compromise its traditions and the spirit of the place. I had to invest in it; but with what? It was, after all, my father's former business and it was his money I was going to have to use. He was going to have to trust me to get it right. It was a risky business and a gamble but I had gambled before on the Tavern. At the Tavern, however, both turnover and profitability were high; at the Coffee House both were low and the risk greater. The business could not mark time, however; I had to move it on. Time and future events would show that if it had not progressed, it would have folded. Firstly, there was some routine investment to be made. The drab green interiors were dispensed with and replaced by a vibrant tan, gold and brown scheme which enhanced the art nouveau fittings. Beautiful handmade cane furniture was purchased that complemented the overall arts and crafts theme. New crockery was required,

**THE KING'S RESTAURANT**
**60 KING STREET, KNUTSFORD, CHESHIRE**
**Tel.: 3060**

**LUNCH 12-00 p.m. to 2-0 p.m. BAR OPEN UNTIL 3-0 p.m.**

**APPETISERS**

| | |
|---|---|
| Melon in Season | 25p |
| Soup of the Day with roll and butter | 15p |
| Fruit Juices | 13p |
| Liver Pate served with buttered Toast | 30p |
| Prawn Cocktail | 35p |

**FROM THE GRILL AND SERVED IN THE GREEN GASKELL ROOM**

| | |
|---|---|
| Grilled Rump Steak | 95p |
| Grilled Fillet Steak | 110p |
| Grilled Pork Chops | 75p |
| Grilled Lamb Cutlets | 70p |
| Grilled Gammon Steaks with Pineapple | 75p |
| Grilled Halibut with Tartare Sauce | 80p |

All the above dishes from the Grill are served with French Fried Potatoes and garnished with grilled Mushroom and Tomato.

or

any one of the following side salads:—

| | |
|---|---|
| Onion Rings in Anchovy Dressing | 15p |
| Tossed Mixed Salad with chopped hard boiled egg | 15p |
| Tomatoes stuffed with diced cucumber in mayonnaise | 15p |

**ENGLISH COLD BUFFET — RED GALSWORTHY ROOM**

We invite you to make your selection from the thirty or so cold dishes. These feature many old English Savoury favourites, to be enjoyed with salad accompaniment. ... 87p

**SWEETS FROM THE TROLLEY**

We will be delighted to bring the sweet trolley to your table. From it we offer you a selection of Gateaux, Fresh Fruit Salad and Trifle from The Fresh Fruit Basket. ... 25p

**BERTORELLI CONTINENTAL ICE CREAM**

| | |
|---|---|
| Praline Dairy Ice Cream | 15p |
| Chocolat-Menthe Dairy Ice Cream | 20p |
| Chocolate Semi-Freddo | 25p |
| Orange Surprise | 25p |
| Mela Stregata | 25p |

A full description of these Ice Creams is on your table.

**ENGLISH CHEESEBOARD**

The Cheeseboard features a variety of English Cheeses and may be viewed from the Trolley. Price including Biscuits and Butter from ... 20p

**COFFEE**

| | |
|---|---|
| Kenco Coffee, per cup with cream or black | 10p |
| Kenco Coffee, per pot, per person | 20p |

**MINIMUM CHARGE PER PERSON DURING LUNCH 70p**

All prices inclusive of 10% V.A.T.
No service charge has been levied and is optional

this time in the KCH livery. In the kitchen, bains-marie were introduced along with a replacement and most-expensive slicing machine.

At first no attempt was made to increase prices; decimalisation was shortly going to take care of this. The time was the late 1960s and the early 1970s and a cup of coffee was one shilling and sixpence (7p in today's money). Lunch (please refrain from smiling) was six shillings and sixpence (33p) for three courses. This has to be taken into context. As yet, dishwashing machines, cold rooms and refrigeration, stainless-steel cookers and much more were things of the future. The whole kitchen itself was hugely unhygienic, with both walls and floors in need of tiling. Fortunately, at that moment in time, the health, hygiene and safety people were not so attentive; maybe they understood the problems of what was something of an institution and were kind to us or, at least, patient. Worst of all, though, was the plague of cockroaches that I inherited. To switch the kitchen lights on suddenly at midnight meant seeing a black mass of little beasts scuttle away, seemingly in a flash. With the splendid help of Rentokil we eventually rid ourselves of the infestation. Until then, my

*The Kings Restaurant menu*

great dread was for one to pop out of the spout of a pot of tea and into some poor unsuspecting old lady's cup.

By far the best way of increasing turnover and profit was through the letting of the hotel's few bedrooms. Father had entered into a contract with the North Western Gas Board, which guaranteed that the rooms would be filled most weeks of the year from Monday to Thursday by young trainee employees. This was at the princely sum of £2 per night per room. Again, please consider that this was the 1960s and £1 the rough equivalent of £20 or more today. This was a silly price and I cancelled the contract. I then did a fairly awful thing and converted the glorious old ballroom and exhibition room into five further bedrooms but not before ensuring that the partitions were of wood and plaster build and could be taken down again if necessary. I had sympathy with the Gas Board, whose training centre was at nearby Mere; they subsequently moved on and the building is now the Mere Court Hotel. I am completely convinced that it does not cater for young lively training gas-board employees, whose nocturnal activities included placing the Coffee House's stuffed crocodile in each

*The Kings Restaurant wine list*

## Wine List

| Bin No. | CHAMPAGNE | Bott. | ½ Bott. |
|---|---|---|---|
| 1 | Santelle | £4-25 | £2-20 |
| 2 | Moet et Chandon N.V. | £4-50 | £2-30 |
| 3 | — | | |

| | SPARKLING WINE | | |
|---|---|---|---|
| 4 | Gancia Spumante | £2-00 | £1-05 |
| 5 | Deinhards Cabinet Sekt | £2-50 | — |
| 6 | Deinhards Sparkling Moselle | £2-50 | — |

| | RED BORDEAUX—CLARET | | |
|---|---|---|---|
| 8 | Mouton Cadet. Selection Baron Phillipe de Rothschild 1966 | £2-10 | £1-10 |
| 9 | Château St. Martin 1967 Medoc (French Bottled) | £2-25 | £1-20 |
| 10 | Château Lacroix, St. Emilion 1967 (French Bottled) | £2-30 | £1-25 |
| 11 | Château Meyney, St. Estéphe 1964 (French Bottled) | £2-50 | £1-30 |
| 12 | Château Prieure Lichine 4th Growth Margaux 1966 Château Bottled | £5-25 | — |

| | WHITE BORDEAUX | | |
|---|---|---|---|
| 14 | Dry Graves | £1-45 | 80 |
| 15 | La Maison Blanche Sauternes | £1-60 | 85 |
| 16 | Barsac | £1-70 | 90 |

| | RED BURGUNDY | | |
|---|---|---|---|
| 18 | Beaujolais 1971 | £2-05 | £1-10 |
| 19 | Volnay 1969 | £2-70 | £1-40 |
| 20 | Gevrey Chambertin 1969 | £2-80 | £1-45 |
| 21 | Nuits St. Georges 1970 | £2-90 | £1-50 |
| 22 | Beaune Greves, Calvet (French Bottled) 1966 | £3-90 | |

| | WHITE BURGUNDY | | |
|---|---|---|---|
| 24 | Chablis 1971 | £2-05 | £1-05 |
| 25 | Pouilly Fuisse 1971 | £2-10 | £1-10 |
| 26 | Chassagne Montrachet 1969 | £2-40 | £1-25 |

| Bin No. | HOCK | Bott | ½ Bott. |
|---|---|---|---|
| 28 | Rudesheimer Rosengarten 1970/72 | £1-70 | 90 |
| 29 | Dorf Johanisberger Langenbach 1970 | £1-95 | £1-00 |
| 30 | Liebfraumilch "Blue Nun" 1970 | £2-35 | £1-25 |

| | MOSELLE | | |
|---|---|---|---|
| 32 | Moselblumchen | £1-50 | 80 |
| 33 | Piesporter Michelsberg 1970/72 | £1-80 | 95 |

| | RHONE | | |
|---|---|---|---|
| 34 | Chateauneuf du Pape 1971 | £2-00 | £1-05 |

| | LOIRE | | |
|---|---|---|---|
| 35 | Muscadet | £1-45 | 80 |

| | ALSATIAN | | |
|---|---|---|---|
| 36 | Sylvaner, French Bottled Jos Meyer | £1-70 | 90 |
| 37 | Gewurztraminer, French Bottled Jos Meyer | £2-10 | £1-10 |

| | ITALIAN | | |
|---|---|---|---|
| 38 | Soave Bolla | £1-80 | £1-00 |
| 39 | Valpolicella, Bolla | £1-80 | £1-00 |
| 40 | Chianti Ruffino Red, Whicker Flasks | £2-05 | £1-10 |
| 41 | Toscano Bianco, Ruffino White | £2-05 | £1-10 |

| | AUSTRIAN | | |
|---|---|---|---|
| 42 | Kamper Reisling | £1-15 | 60 |

| | PORTUGUESE | | |
|---|---|---|---|
| 43 | Mateus Rose, Petillant Bottled in Portugal | £1-85 | £1-05 |
| 44 | Avcleda, Vinho Verde Petillant (Estate Bottled) | £1-50 | 80 |

**CARAFE WINE**
Hirondelle Red, White, Rose—per Carafe £1-10, per ½ Carafe 65p.
Carousel Sweet White—per Carafe £1-10, per ½ Carafe 65p.

**WINE BY THE GLASS**
Red, Medium White, Sweet White and Rose—per Glass 25p.

Wines supplied from the cellars of Bass-Charrington (North West) Ltd.

other's beds, Godfather-style. It was easy to detect in which room the poor reptile reclined by the trail of sawdust that led from the empty wall where it had hung to the bedroom door. Towards the end it was becoming so emaciated that it looked like a huge empty gentleman's wallet.

With sufficient enough bedrooms to make a substantial increase in the turnover via the introduction of a higher-priced tariff, I could now have gone public and catered for upmarket but occasional business; this would have been a slow process and in need of costly publicity material and advertising. I took the easy way out and entered into an agreement with the then thoroughly successful Nuclear Power Group, which was partly located at nearby Booths Hall and which overlooked Toft Cricket Club's ground. The company was extremely happy to pay the new prices and to have somewhere reasonably sophisticated, adjacent, fairly historic and all theirs. Although the business did not serve dinner, the residents were delighted to be recommended to and to be given special attention at our related business at the Tavern. All our rooms were occupied again from Monday to Thursday, leaving me to coach the Toft CC Junior Section on Saturday mornings, a liberty this, as Saturday was a very busy day at the Coffee House. We were closed on Sundays, which meant more cricket, as Toft were then heavily involved in the National Village Knockout Cup.

We were happy and pleased to be asked to entertain and cater for the needs of some of the Nuclear Power Group's more prestigious clientele. On one such occasion we were asked to pay very special attention to an Italian gentleman who turned out to be no less than the professor of astronomy at Pisa University and was thus occupying the chair that the great and glorious Galileo himself had occupied so may years before. He had been asked to lecture the scientists at Radbroke Hall. What an honour,

*The rear of the entrance to the Galsworthy Room* with the *bronze statue 'Le Faucheur' by Gaudez. This was stolen shortly after the departure of the Howard family, the lesson being that staff who live in do not exercise the same care with property. The statue has never been recovered.*

of course, this was for us! I was duly briefed by the company and further pressed to attend to the professor's every need. All stops were to be pulled. With the Coffee House closed during the evening, the establishment was, of course, quiet. I was, as usual, involved with the books, ledgers and so on, and needed only one member of staff, to act as receptionist and general factotum. To do this, I employed part-time Knutsford ladies who were attractive, well-mannered, intelligent and with plenty of common sense. They were ladies whom I always knew fairly well and were, anyway, daytime customers of the Coffee House. Just a little pocket money and to get out of the house was their small need. One such lady was Jean who was on duty on this occasion and my brief to her was to give the professor everything he asked for and to pander to his every whim. On arriving and prior to going out for dinner that evening, he had asked for a bottle of brandy and glasses to be taken up to him after he had bathed and dressed. I must point out at this juncture that the gentleman bore no resemblance whatsoever to the average person's immediate vision of a learned professor – not long-haired and bearded but the most handsome of Italian men imaginable. Good heavens! Was he good-looking and didn't he just know it! I did not see Jean wilt in his presence and she was duly last seen disappearing upstairs with her tray of brandy. Be assured that I was not counting in minutes but I did notice, after fifteen minutes or so, that she had not reappeared. Several minutes

*The long wall in the Galsworthy Room*

later she did, looking slightly dishevelled, highly-coloured and extremely agitated. It appeared that in following my brief to the letter to take great care of the fellow, she had been asked if she would care to join him in a glass of brandy, sit on the edge of the bed where he joined her and engaged her seemingly in harmless conversation which lasted some ten minutes. Then, without much ado, he pushed her back on the bed and attempted to kiss her. Jean, the sweet innocent housewife and mother that she was, duly panicked and fled the scene, believing that accepting the amorous advances of the professor was not quite within the remit of her instructions

– for queen and country, maybe, but not for the Nuclear Power Group nor for the Kings Coffee House. Of course, we made nothing of it. The professor appeared later, immaculately turned out, as smooth and unruffled as ever. On many occasions over the years, whenever Jean and I bumped into each other, we always exchanged jests and I pulled her leg unmercifully. One conclusion that can be drawn with regard to Italian professors is that professors they may well be, but first and foremost they are essentially Italian. Thank heavens!

To revert to much more serious matters, and a very sad one for my mother, my family and myself, my father's cancerous condition was worsening. His tumour must have been a terrible thing for him to have to endure. His speech was so badly affected that he could hardly communicate and he was now for the most part bed-bound. My mother and I were doing our best to look after him, which was difficult during the working day, when we were both involved with running the business – myself front of house and she managing the kitchen. My father's mental torment must have been a terrible thing to have to bear. It was to manifest itself one working day. I had managed to slide away from the counter during a busy lunch hour to see how he was, only to find that he wasn't in his bedroom but, on hearing a splashing noise in the next-door bathroom, I entered to find him naked and trying to submerge himself in a very full bath

*A corner of the Galsworthy Room.*

of water. Had I been ten minutes or so later, he would have drowned himself. I pulled him out of the bath, wrapped him in a blanket and sat down on the staircase step with him, where we both cried our hearts out, he in recognising the hopelessness of his condition, myself with terrible pity for a father I loved dearly. He was very shortly admitted to hospital and died there in great pain within a few weeks. So awful was his death that I admit I wished that I had been twenty minutes later going upstairs that day to see him. The piteous scene at his hospital bedside will live long in my memory. So died a man who had once been described as 'the whitest man in Knutsford'.

It was time to put this dreadful time for the family behind us and for me to get on with the process of reinvigorating the Kings Coffee House. I was desperately keen to re-establish its links with its artistic past. These had eroded over the years through the ageing process of the Wilson Hall sisters. The music room had variously been Knutsford Council Chamber, Masonic Lodge and now the Tavern restaurant. The library and reading room had become the residents' lounge and I criminally had converted the upstairs exhibition room cum ballroom into bedrooms. Now I had a yen to hang paintings in the Misses Wilson-Hall tradition, both ladies having been well recognised and much-exhibited painters in their day. To do this, I made contact with various artistic groups and societies in the North West, mainly in Cheshire, and invited them to hang their works in the coffee room, a room which everybody had to pass through. This worked well for a while and culminated in an exhibition given by members of the Augustine Studio, a very fine London colony of supreme artists who had been recommended to me by my uncle, former major, Kenneth Lee, then in business in Berkeley Square in the capital. I was right to accept his recommendation, for they exhibited a collection of paintings, sculpture, handmade gold and silver objects, pottery and jewellery, the likes of which I had rarely seen before. The craftsmanship was breathtakingly beautiful and it was a privilege to display the work. That they came to Knutsford was in no small measure due

to the former reputation of the Kings Coffee House and, of course, its charm. This dalliance with painting was to lead me further in my desire to resurrect the link the Kings Coffee House had with the fine arts; music also was to be not too far away in my thoughts.

The high-quality objects that the Augustine Studios brought to the Coffee House were, again, to act as a stimulus. My responsibility was to be able to display them to their best advantage and I had, of course, given due consideration to the matter. Richard Watt had designed and built as part of the facade of the building the most beautiful bow window imaginable. It projected into the main street and is considered the best in Knutsford, if not Cheshire. Originally it had shown the patisserie that had been produced in the business's model bakery. When that was demolished, no further commercial use had been found for it and it became a worthy home for the Studio's hand-crafted artwork.

The whole process of window display had the effect of rekindling my now long-gone retailing instincts. I had the opportunity to again don the former retail-buying and selling cap that I had worn for Harrods and which I had tossed away to enter the restaurant trade. This window and another window in the Coffee House courtyard that had lain fallow for so many years were quite patently the most advantageous areas in which to show fine merchandise. It was obvious to me,

***The Giftique,*** *1970-1974, was a boutique offering original and carefully bought giftware, much of it from China, Russia, Denmark and Sweden. It closed in 1974 with the advent of the La Belle Epoque, after which it was later to display wedding gowns*

taking a leaf from the Augustine Studios book, that art-related items that were attractive, of quality and originality without being overpriced, could be displayed to good effect and would interest a mainly feminine and largely already-captive clientele. In short, this was to be gift-type merchandise. I had myself an instant upmarket

gift shop to which I gave the hugely unimaginative name 'The Giftique' – an easy name to remember if you are trying to locate a gift shop. My logo was a black silhouette of the building on a white ground. You knew immediately where the goods in the bag came from.

The old Harrods buying principles were then put to good use, that is to search high and low and, if necessary, far afield for merchandise that was not available at or not considered by other outlets within preferably a 50-mile radius. I was soon on the pre-seasonal road to trade fairs in London, Harrogate, Birmingham and elsewhere. Not for me fine Staffordshire porcelain or crystal glassware and the like, which could be found in Knutsford and other local towns ad nauseam. I sought out studio glass and ceramics, sculptural bronzes, high-quality continental jewellery and hung the walls with quality prints. Where a noted manufacturer was not represented locally, I did take advantage, however. For instance, it was incredible that Moorcroft pottery was not available and I was able to gorge on it; I wish now that I had held onto it as an investment. This merchandise, of course, was all being purchased with the profits from the hotel and restaurant; I trod a fine line but the portents then were good!

It was by now high time to grasp the Coffee House nettle fully and to bring it forward to meet the requirements of that period's needs and demands, that without losing the charm of the place. In fact, everything was done so as to enhance its exquisite art nouveau and arts and crafts decor and traditions. Businesses of this type could succeed if tuned to the pace of the modern day. 'Bettys', that splendid group of Yorkshire tea and coffee houses, is the most prominent example; Swiss-orientated, they are able to bake their own exquisite patisserie. Our model bakery was long gone and we had been buying cakes from a local competitor and selling them at little profit. The fine chocolate, also, turned over very slowly. The 32-pence three-course lunch was suicidal and had to go and, being unlicensed, we could not serve a civilised glass of wine. I applied for and easily obtained a licence to sell wines and spirits. But where and what from? Sadly, out went the cake and chocolate counter and in its place we built a good-looking dispense bar, craftmanship made, that was moulded in the arts and crafts style and totally sympathetic to Watt's original interior design.

It was difficult for me to refrain from buying the finest wines but there would have been little demand for them. Not a lot of wines are consumed in the lunch period and the Coffee House was not in the business-expense bracket. Our ladies, forever careful, would, it was predicted, permit themselves just a glass of wine or sherry. The wine list was therefore limited to the more popular and reasonably priced wines, although I did stock the odd good bottle for the very occasional wine buff. To the horror of my regular customers, who knew a bargain when they saw one, I dropped the 32-pence lunch but was unable to replace it with a modern and more sophisticated menu. My cook was a lovely middle-aged lady who had cooked in her own way all her life and would have found 'new-fangled' recipes difficult to cope with; she was, anyway, part and parcel of the establishment, so we were unable to go the full hog. The menu was largely made up of light meals of grilled food and salads. The soups and puddings remained 'wholesome' but priced separately. All was now in place and we were all systems go. It was, however, a high-risk programme that I had adopted; I was treading a fine and protracted financial line and keeping a lot of monetary balls in the air at one time. Although the swinging sixties had shortly ended, there was no reason to believe that the seventies would not also be of the swinging variety and I needed the buoyant trading period to continue, to finance my ventures. It was not to be.

Disaster struck with a vengeance and very quickly; we must have been blind not to see it coming. The economic and political situation under the governance of Ted Heath's Conservative government was to prove inept under the challenge of the trade unions. The country's electricity network was vulnerable to mechanical failure and industrial action. In December 1973 hospitals were being forced to function on batteries and candles during a 'work to rule' strike by the mineworkers' union. At the same

## *Hotels*

## HUMPHREY LYTTELTON finds a delightful coffee house in KNUTSFORD – an amazing jumble of styles and functions.

Richard Harding Watt was what an American with an ear for a pun would probably call a 'knut'. Living in Knutsford around the turn of the century, he performed a peculiarly English double role: on the one hand he was a successful and prosperous glove-merchant and on the other a passionate amateur artist and designer, with a sideline in philanthropy and speeding in his horse-drawn carriage. When several Georgian neo-classical public buildings in nearby Manchester were demolished – St Peter's Church, the Royal Infirmary – he had the stone brought across and dumped in great heaps all over Knutsford while he designed buildings which incorporated his feeling for Classicism, Italian architecture and Art Nouveau, in which he was a forerunner. Undeterred when his first buildings succumbed to the laws of gravity and toppled down a hill, he went on, with more expert engineering advice, to build a row of mansions on the outer fringe of the town and a coffee house in its centre. As if blending the classical, the Italian and the nouveau were not enough, he decided that his King's Coffee House should be a memorial to the novelist Mrs Gaskell whose *Cranford* was a portrait of Knutsford in the nineteenth century.

Here we are, you may well be saying, knee-deep in industrial, architectural and literary history, none of which is noticeably relevant to the matter in hand specified by the word HOTELS at the head of this column. Bear with me a bit longer and light will dawn. Richard Harding Watt's chief buyer in the glove business was a Mr Howard, who used to accompany Watt on his jaunts to Italy – presumably taking care of business while the head of the firm was gadding about looking at architecture. Mr Howard's grandson and his wife now own the **King's Coffee House**, 60 King Street (Knutsford 3060) and, after a lapse of time since the days when it harboured famous literary figures like John Galsworthy, have now reopened its residential side. In effect, the building now operates on three fronts – as a coffee house where the townsfolk call in for coffee or a plain lunch and to rest weary feet, as a small hotel with simply-furnished but very comfortable rooms and a cosy TV lounge, and as a restaurant called The Tavern which Mr and Mrs Howard run as a separate entity in a big room designed by Watt as a music and recreation room to keep his workers out of the pubs.

Having an early engagement in Liverpool thirty miles away, I did not have time to do full justice to the food at the Tavern restaurant, where the choice is between a selection of hot dishes or a forage-for-yourself Danish salad table priced at £1·50 for as much as you can eat from the fish and meat courses. You perch on tall chairs around high tables designed to counteract the feeling of Lilliputian inferiority which might otherwise be induced by the enormously high ceiling. Even a fleeting visit was enough to show that this informal setting with strong Continental associations is just right for this adjunct to the Coffee House.

It is, after all, a Continental feeling that one gets from the intriguing jumble of styles and functions blended together in this extraordinary building. All sorts of things contribute – the mixture of mosaic tiles, Victorian paintings, curly bamboo-work screens, marble-topped tables and ornaments from everywhere and anywhere which Mr Howard has thankfully preserved to achieve a sort of diverse unity. There are no doubt more well-appointed, luxurious, modernised and generally streamlined hotels in the surrounds of Manchester, but few will make you feel more welcome and none will provide so many talking points as you eat your breakfast looking out at the extraordinary memorial tower to Elizabeth Gaskell, or spot strange bits of historical information chiselled on the reassembled blocks of Manchester stone round the entrance. Fascinating is the word.

*The Humphrey Lyttleton review of the Kings Coffee House in Harpers and Queen magazine 1973* time an oil crisis had worsened the situation and had caused Heath to impose a prices and incomes policy to cap rising inflation. The unions had resisted and a series of further strikes forced him to declare the three-day working week from January 1974, to nurse the electricity system through the crisis. It is hard for anyone today to imagine how dreadful this all was. Unemployment became high as businesses cut their staff in an effort to keep afloat. Recklessly, I refused to do this. In an attempt to remain loyal to both my customers and my staff, I chose to try to keep functioning as if all were normal. Businesses throughout the country started to crash by the thousands. Small businesses in particular were badly affected; the cafe trade was savaged and both my rivals in the town were forced to close, one of them never to reopen. The Coffee House building complex, including the Tavern restaurant, was and is huge, and the heating and lighting bills were enormous. Nevertheless, I chose not to shorten my opening hours and I remained open despite being without heat and light for days on end. My elderly and mainly feminine clientele could be forgiven for not wishing to sit in a cold and darkened restaurant, so they stayed away. My giftware trade suffered accordingly, as there were fewer ladies about, to be tempted, and less money for such luxuries. My bedrooms were empty, as my eggs were all confined to the business basket and the Nuclear Power Group was pulling its horns in. All this was not helped by the introduction in 1971 of decimalisation which further added to already raging inflation. My feminine clientele had difficulty in coming to terms with the fact that the old one shilling and three pence cup of coffee, or 6p decimal, was suddenly 10p. I reckoned that decimalisation meant a 50% increase across the trading board. Now you can pay £3 per cup of coffee. Luckily we avoided the introduction of the euro, which saw prices rise overnight in Europe.

My high-risk investment in the business was soon to prove a threat to its very existence. The necessary period of consolidation was no longer available. Accounts became harder to pay and took longer to do so. Tradespeople were in the same boat and in desperate need of their money. I had no capital to invest in new stock for the gift shop, which meant fatal stagnation. In short, I was staring disaster in the face and had to do something fairly drastic and rapidly at that. The very obvious way out was to substantially increase my turnover without increasing my costs too much. But how? I could not do that within the confines and structured style of the existing business. It was hugely apparent that the way to do this was to increase the hours of opening. In short, to open in the evenings. I had never contemplated doing this, as I would have placed myself in competition with my ex-wife who was trading upstairs at the Tavern Restaurant. I had had no wish to hazard her operation or threaten what was proving to be her expensive lifestyle. Now I really had no other recourse; she would have been more under threat had I gone to the wall and had to surrender the head lease to the Knutsford Council. Another landlord would not have been so sympathetic. I was, after all, still asking her for the miniscule rent that my father had kindly requested from me.

I had much missed the excitement of my days at the Tavern; they had been lovely working-days. The restaurant had been very successful and it had been hard to say goodbye to it. The Coffee House had provided me with a further challenge, as it had been much harder to change a business that had become so rooted in tradition than it was to create one from nothing, as was the case with the Tavern. I had little doubt that the Coffee House that my father took on in the fifties and managed through the sixties would never have survived the winter of 1973-74. Now my luck had changed. We had come very far and stood at the threshold of something that could prove to be very good indeed. I was not going to lose the business that I had toiled to change and in which I had invested so much time and capital. I now relished the prospect of again trading in the evening and meeting the needs of a wider, more affluent and demanding clientele. I knew this type of market like the back of my hand; it was one that I had learnt during my buying days and earlier trading, with Harrods. I relished the thought of being once again involved in the buying of fine wines. To get to the crude point, customers in the evenings spend more on food and drink over a longer period than those at lunchtime do. The interiors of the Coffee House would be even more interesting and beautiful when lit at night. Customers would be more thrilled by its splendid art nouveau/arts and crafts decor. There would be little need of further investment in the front of the restaurant. We were licensed, had a bar and smart furniture. The kitchen still presented many problems in terms of equipment and would have to be adapted to meet the needs of the new chefs who would prepare the food for whatever cuisine was chosen. But what cuisine? For me this had long been obvious. Here, in the middle of the main street of a lovely old market town stood this amazing Italianate building. What better cuisine than Italian? I have to remind the reader at this point that Italian food 50-odd years ago was not commonplace in the British high street. Certainly there was a presence in the big cities but it would definitely be the first in Knutsford; nowadays, at the last count, there are three. This would be the only Italian restaurant in the country that traded in an Italianate building; it made very good sense. The quality of the building, particularly its interiors, dictated that the food served should also be of the highest quality. I would never ever have chosen to serve pizzas, although they doubtless would have proved to be a raging success. The pizza-house chains of restaurants were still not yet evident in the towns; we maybe could have been the first. No, certainly not a pizzeria or trattoria; the latter also would have been a sure-fire winner. Either would have been easier to manage, easier to operate and less demanding all round. Not for me, though, the easy way! I just had to make life difficult for myself. I did not want to court the popular trade; I wanted to be different, however hard. It would have to be a ristorante, and as unique and original as was ever possible.

I decided to endeavour to create a menu from the classic cuisines of the four north-Italian provinces – the meat dishes from Emilia-Romagna, the vegetable dishes from Tuscany, the fish from Veneto, the sweet dishes and other refined foods from Lombardy. I took myself off on a whirlwind tour of the great capital cities of Bologna, Florence, Venice and Milan, sampling the food, making numerous notes, absorbing the heady atmosphere of their best restaurants, believing the cost would be handsomely repaid in due course. At the same time, I was placing equally costly personal advertisements in the relevant Italian papers, needing to attract the attention and interest of an entrepreneurial Italian superman who would give the project a very necessary authenticity. This had been an essential ingredient in establishing the Tavern as a 'pukka' Danish restaurant. His main job of work, initially, would be to recruit an Italian crew, including chefs. I had plenty of bedrooms to accommodate them, with some left over for commercial use. It all depended on the right guy turning up. He didn't and time was running out. My only other recourse, then, was to tap into an increasing Italian catering population in the UK. The 'Mario and Franco' group of trattorias had by now established themselves in British cities and had gained a good reputation. I took myself off in an attempt to poach one of their bright and hopefully enterprising managers and I succeeded in interesting a certain Gianni who looked the part and who, I thought, would be splendid. After some negotiation we agreed to proceed but the very next day his English wife told him she was not prepared to move to Knutsford. Good heavens! This is a town in which people are prepared to spend a fortune to come and live. Maybe I was wrong in my judgment; he certainly was. A few years later, with La Belle Epoque up and running smoothly as one of the leading restaurants in the north of England, I bumped into him in his then role of manager of a Manchester bar. He confessed with great sadness to having made the biggest mistake of his life.

I really was in trouble now. Time was of the essence and I was certainly running out of it. Then my luck changed. For many months, on most Saturday afternoons, a small family sat at a corner table adjoining the bar; they were Malcolm and Dominique Mooney with their six-month-old little boy, Laurent. The Mooneys owned a very successful and authentically French bistro in a precinct in nearby Hale Barns, called The Borsalino. He was English and she Norman

61

French from Caen. We obviously had restaurant interests in common, got on well and talked business. I had for many months been outlining to him my plans for my classic Italian restaurant and he was so enthusiastic that he went so far as to venture that, if I ever changed my mind, would I consider bringing him into the business as a partner, as he believed that the building would make an equally beautiful French restaurant. The dire situation I was now in left me little alternative other than to contact him with a view to doing just that. The Kings Coffee House was not to become the first Italian restaurant in Knutsford. That honour went to Est Est Est, which opened in 1988, whose brilliant creator Derek Lilley went on to build a chain of unique and classy restaurants. Thus was La Belle Epoque born and it would go on to mature into a highly reputable and renowned French restaurant.

# The La Belle Epoque

Malcolm Mooney was quite a character, being bright, progressive, enthusiastic and ambitious. I am sure I am right in saying that he owned a menswear boutique in an area of Manchester then known as 'the village', which was behind Deansgate and roughly to the rear of Kendal Milne. His colleague in the business was none other than the young George Best, the celebrated northern Irishman, playing wonderful football in another great Manchester United Team. He, of course, was building a reputation as a bon viveur, if that is the way to describe George. George and Malcolm got on extremely well together, so well, in fact, that Malcolm became George's very first manager. His description of life with Best in that capacity was simply riotous, as George's services seemed to be in great demand the length and breadth of Europe, and not in his capacity as footballer. His exploits attracted the covetous attention of Manchester's not so illustrious smart set, including individuals who desired a slice of the Best lifestyle, many jostling Malcolm for his position as his manager. He found this exasperating and very wearing, so much so that, in total disgust, he relinquished his managerial role. He and Dominique then opened the Borsalino, a truly French bistro.

Not too much time was needed to get the Belle Epoque business underway – a little fine tuning here and there in the front of the house, particularly with the lighting, the restaurant never ever having been utilised in the evening before. The kitchen, however, did need bringing up to date. Another oven was purchased in addition to the one I had recently bought, a cold room was built and dishwashing machines introduced. Most costly of all was the need to conform to hygiene regulations and much tiling needed to be done to walls and floors. The modus operandi at the newly created La Belle Epoque was for Dominique Mooney to establish the classic French cuisine. Soon we had engaged the services of a group of splendid local young ladies who enjoyed a country lifestyle and needed a vehicle in which to express their talent for cooking; in some instances to earn a little extra to keep a pony. All were fine cooks with cordon bleu training and all with experience in other good local restaurants. They were, of course, taking over the duties of the former Coffee House cooks, who had retired, realising that change was inevitable and who, anyway, were of retirement age; mercifully, there were no sackings. The new cooks were, of course, in no need of lessons in how to prepare French cuisine. Dominique was there to establish the overall French style of the

Dominique & Malcolm Mooney & John Howard
requests the pleasure of the company of

to a dinner to celebrate the opening of

# LA BELLE EPOQUE

restaurant français

60 King Street, Knutsford, at      p.m. Sunday, 8th September

R.S.V.P.

*The invitation to the launch of the La Belle Epoque – 8 September 1973*

menu. In addition, we took on board a bevy of young attractive French girls, whom we could easily accommodate and employ as waitresses The essentially French atmosphere was thus realised, with Dominique working in Knutsford while Malcolm had to remain at the Borsalino to ensure its continued success. I managed front of house, customer accounts and the wine buying and service in La Belle Epoque.

Dominique and Malcolm lived in nearby High Legh, roughly midway between the two restaurants. With her kitchen-management duties over by 10.00pm, Dominique would leave to go home and ensure that the very young Laurent was well seen to. Malcolm, of course, had to put the Borsalino to bed, which invariably was very late. Naturally, he wanted to see how we were progressing with the new restaurant and he would call on his way home, which meant a roundabout journey. We would chat for half an hour about the evening's business and who had been in that he knew; he would then proceed on his way home. Then tragedy occurred. Just nine weeks after we had opened the La Belle Epoque, he was making the very same way home via Mere corner, with a green light in his favour, when a lorry driven by a drunken driver drove his vehicle through a red light and struck Malcolm's car broadside on, killing him instantly. Sadly, I had been the last person to see him alive. So ended a very brief but exhilarating relationship with a man whom I found to be inspirational. The funeral took place in Knutsford cemetery on a cold bleak November afternoon. I was one of the four pallbearers who carried his coffin; at the rear end were a wealthy businessman and old customer and a former Cheshire County Rugby

Union three-quarter. I took the right-hand front corner and linked arms with the man on the left who happened to be George Best. This was the nearest I would ever get to a footballing hero of mine. How I wish it could have been in less tragic circumstances! It was all so horribly surreal. Poor Malcolm was laid to rest in a quiet far corner of the cemetery seemingly, but I am sure not, forgotten as the years have rolled on.

I am sure that from the moment of Malcolm's death Dominique felt that the move from the Borsalino to the La Belle Epoque was ill fated and, with the Borsalino now without its charismatic figurehead, she felt the need to take over the front of restaurant duties there. However difficult that was under the circumstances, she bravely took the helm. Her good close friend and fellow director, Nicole Guerin, joined me in Knutsford to maintain the French style. Dominique eventually married again, this time a fellow countryman, and

*The La Belle Epoque wine list 1985. A fine example of the artwork provided by the late Keith Mooney's printing business in Colne, Lancashire. A former sommelier declared that the wines on offer were equal to, if not better than, those of the Manchester Midland Hotel's fine French restaurant.*

moved back to France and to live in Paris. The Borsalino closed its doors, to become a dear memory as possibly the last of the truly French bistros, as we have now been swamped by a plethora of Italian restaurants. I remained at the front of the La Belle Epoque with that wonderful crew of cordon-bleu cooks continuing to present truly excellent classic French cuisine, the restaurant very soon rightfully earning its entry into the almighty Good Food Guide.

Before Malcolm was killed, his killer incidentally only receiving a six-month prison sentence for his heinous crime, we had discussed the possibility of presenting classical music in the restaurant on a once-a-month basis, along with an equally classic French meal of several courses. We knew that the block of bedrooms that I had constructed a few short years earlier in the concert/exhibition room could quite easily be taken down and become a venue for musical events. I was thrilled at the thought of music again returning to the lovely old building. The artistic wheel would then have turned a full circle. All would be as Richard Harding Watt and the Miss Wilsons had intended more

*Cheshire Life feature* – September 1974

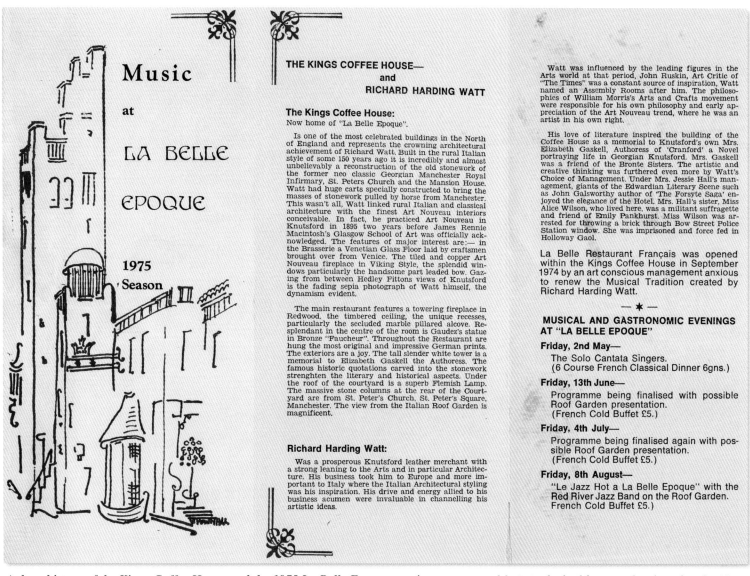

# Music
## at
## LA BELLE
## EPOQUE

**1975 Season**

### THE KINGS COFFEE HOUSE—
### and
### RICHARD HARDING WATT

**The Kings Coffee House:**

Now home of "La Belle Epoque".

Is one of the most celebrated buildings in the North of England and represents the crowning architectural achievement of Richard Watt. Built in the rural Italian style of some 150 years ago it is incredibly and almost unbelievably a reconstruction of the old stonework of the former neo classic Georgian Manchester Royal Infirmary, St. Peters Church and the Mansion House. Watt had huge carts specially constructed to bring the masses of stonework pulled by horse from Manchester. This wasn't all, Watt linked rural Italian and classical architecture with the finest Art Nouveau interiors conceivable. In fact, he practiced Art Nouveau in Knutsford in 1895 two years before James Rennie Macintosh's Glasgow School of Art was officially acknowledged. The features of major interest are:— in the Brasserie a Venetian Glass Floor laid by craftsmen brought over from Venice. The tiled and copper Art Nouveau fireplace in Viking Style, the splendid windows particularly the handsome part leaded bow. Gazing from between Hedley Fittons views of Knutsford is the fading sepia photograph of Watt himself, the dynamism evident.

The main restaurant features a towering fireplace in Redwood, the timbered ceiling, the unique recesses, particularly the secluded marble pillared alcove. Resplendant in the centre of the room is Gaudez's statue in Bronze "Faucheur". Throughout the Restaurant are hung the most original and impressive German prints. The exteriors are a joy. The tall slender white tower is a memorial to Elizabeth Gaskell the Authoress. The famous historic quotations carved into the stonework strenghten the literary and historical aspects. Under the roof of the courtyard is a superb Flemish Lamp. The massive stone columns at the rear of the Courtyard are from St. Peter's Church, St. Peter's Square, Manchester. The view from the Italian Roof Garden is magnificent.

**Richard Harding Watt:**

Was a prosperous Knutsford leather merchant with a strong leaning to the Arts and in particular Architecture. His business took him to Europe and more important to Italy where the Italian Architectural styling was his inspiration. His drive and energy allied to his business acumen were invaluable in channelling his artistic ideas.

Watt was influenced by the leading figures in the Arts world at that period, John Ruskin, Art Critic of "The Times" was a constant source of inspiration, Watt named an Assembly Rooms after him. The philosophies of William Morris's Arts and Crafts movement were responsible for his own philosophy and early appreciation of the Art Nouveau trend, where he was an artist in his own right.

His love of literature inspired the building of the Coffee House as a memorial to Knutsford's own Mrs. Elizabeth Gaskell, Authoress of 'Cranford' a Novel portraying life in Georgian Knutsford. Mrs. Gaskell was a friend of the Bronte Sisters. The artistic and creative thinking was furthered even more by Watt's Choice of Management. Under Mrs. Jessie Hall's management, giants of the Edwardian Literary Scene such as John Galsworthy author of 'The Forsyte Saga' enjoyed the elegance of the Hotel. Mrs. Hall's sister, Miss Alice Wilson, who lived here, was a militant suffragette and friend of Emily Pankhurst. Miss Wilson was arrested for throwing a brick through Bow Street Police Station window. She was imprisoned and force fed in Holloway Gaol.

La Belle Restaurant Français was opened within the Kings Coffee House in September 1974 by an art conscious management anxious to renew the Musical Tradition created by Richard Harding Watt.

— ✱ —

### MUSICAL AND GASTRONOMIC EVENINGS AT "LA BELLE EPOQUE"

**Friday, 2nd May—**
The Solo Cantata Singers.
(6 Course French Classical Dinner 6gns.)

**Friday, 13th June—**
Programme being finalised with possible Roof Garden presentation.
(French Cold Buffet £5.)

**Friday, 4th July—**
Programme being finalised again with possible Roof Garden presentation.
(French Cold Buffet £5.)

**Friday, 8th August—**
"Le Jazz Hot a La Belle Epoque" with the Red River Jazz Band on the Roof Garden.
French Cold Buffet £5.)

*A short history of the Kings Coffee House and the 1975 La Belle Epoque music programme. Music in the building was last heard in the 20s and 30s. The 1975 programme leant towards classical music; later programmes towards more popular music.*

than half a century earlier. The concert room would be restored to its early-20th-century glory. With Malcolm gone, the onus was on me. I cannot for the life of me remember how I came upon

Nicholas and Sally Smith. I needed someone who could take my hand and lead me through what might have been a musical minefield. I am not a music buff but classical music was not exactly

## BRIEF HISTORIES

**Humphrey Lyttleton and His Band**
Toured Britain with Louis Armstrong and the same year toured with Sydney Bechet. 1959 his band toured America with Cannonball Adderley, George Shearing and Thelonius Monk. During the past 18 years he has moved from The New Orleans Style to the forefront of British Jazz with the emphasis on swing. His all star band includes the Saxaphone Stars Kathy Stobart and Bruce Turner.

**Alan Cuckston, Christopher Underwood and Gordon Pullen**
Alan Cuckston needs no introducing to La Belle Epoque he has delighted audiences here with his humour and his performances on Harpsicord and Piano Forte. Christopher Underwood the noted Baritone is no stranger here either. He sang with the Solo Cantata Singers here in May and is joined by Gordon Pullen a Tenor well known in Northern Operatic Circles.

**The Vintage Syncopators**
Are old and trusted friends. They have played their own particular brand of Dixieland Jazz and Comedy in cabaret clubs throughout England, The Continent and North Africa.

**Nicola Gebolys**
Won the British National Piano Playing Competition when she was 13. Then became soloist with the National Youth Orchestra, she made her first appearance at the proms when she was 17 with the Halle Orchestra. She has broadcast with the B.B.C. and played in Germany, Italy, Austria and played Concertos with the leading Symphony Orchestras.

**Chethams Hospital School of Music Chamber Orchestra**
The buildings of the ancient school date back to before 1420. It became Mr. Humphrey Chethams School 'for the sons of honest industrious and painful parents' in 1656. In 1969 it became a specialist school of music. The Chamber Orchestra is a recent addition to the Schools activities. Its fast growing reputation has led to its first concert to Russia, Poland and Scandinavia which commences immediately after their appearance at La Belle Epoque.

**The Red River Jazz Band**
Are a Group of Northern Jazz Musicians playing traditional and main stream music with spirit, drive and with tremendous technical ability. They have played with all the well known British Jazz Musicians.

**Larry Adler**
La Belle Epoque is pleased to welcome the World famous American Harmonica Virtuoso Mr. Larry Adler. Mr. Adler has made concert and TV appearances all over the world. Recently he has built a reputation on International TV for his wit and humour. He is altogether a remarkable entertainer.

**The Alan Fawkes Modern Jazz Quintet**
Alan Fawkes is one of the most highly talented and technically proficient Jazz Musicians in England. His knowledge of his craft and his dedication to it is without question. He is master of his Art on all the Saxophones, Clarinet and Flute. He will appear with a pickup band in October.

**Pepe Martinez**
The Seville born Flamenco Guitarist is numbered among the most eminent in Spain apart from his Solo concert appearances on tour in Europe, he has accompanied the most famous singers and dancers in concert, and the customary private gathering of the Spanish nobility. His music and his life in Seville have been the subject of full length television documentaries on B.B.C.2 and Madrid Television.

**Musical & Gastronomic Evenings**

## Musical and Gastronomic Evenings

### LA BELLE EPOQUE
restaurant francais

**Thursday and Friday, 19th and 20th February**
*Humphrey Lyttleton and his Band*
(5 Course French Regional Dinner £8.50)

**Friday, 12th March**
*A Victorian Evening with Alan Cuckston, Christopher Underwood and Gordon Pullen*
(6 Course French Classic Dinner £7.00)

**Thursday and Friday, 8th and 9th April**
*Jazz with Humour*
*The Vintage Syncopators*
(5 Course French Regional Dinner £6.50)

**Thursday and Friday, 6th and 7th May**
*Piano Recital—Nicola Gebolys plays Chopin, Mozart and the French Composers*
(6 Course French Classic Dinner £7.50)

**Thursday and Friday, 27th and 28th May**
At going to Press it was almost certain that we would be able to book one of the All Time Great Jazz Musicians and Band. Unfortunately this cannot be confirmed until late December. Please await details
(French Cold Buffet £9.50)

**Friday, 2nd July**
*Chethams Hospital School of Music Chamber Orchestra (Prior to their tour of Russia) on the Roof Garden*
(French Cold Buffet £7.50)

**Thursday and Friday, 5th and 6th August**
*'Le Jazz Hot a la Belle Epoque'*
*Red River Jazz Band*
*on the Roof Garden*
(French Cold Buffet £6.50)

*The 1976 Musical and Gastronomic Evening programme*

foreign to me. In the past I had attended Hallé orchestral concerts in Manchester's Free Trade Hall. I had also gone along to concerts given by students at the Royal Northern College of Music, where a wonderful array of talented young musicians perfected their skills. This must have been the path that led me to the Smiths, who, Nick Smith in particular, were highly involved and in

## LA BELLE EPOQUE

restaurant francais

The Kings Coffee House.
Is one of the most celebrated buildings in the North of England and represents the crowning architectural achievement of Richard Watt. Built in the rural Italian style of some 150 years ago it is incredibly and almost unbelievably a reconstruction of the old stonework of the former neo-classic Georgian Manchester Royal Infirmary, St. Peter's Church and the Mansion House. Watt had huge carts specially constructed to bring the masses of stonework pulled by horse from Manchester. This wasn't all, Watt linked rural Italian and classical architecture with the finest Art Nouveau interiors conceivable. In fact, he practiced Art Nouveau in Knutsford in 1895 two years before James Rennie, Macintosh's Glasgow School of Art was officially acknowledged. The features of major interest are:— in the Brasserie a Venetian Glass Floor laid by craftsman brought over from Venice. The tiled and copper Art Nouveau fireplace in Viking Style, the splendid windows particularly the handsome part leaded bow. Gazing from between Hedley Fittons views of Knutsford is the fading sepia photograph of Watt himself, the dynamism evident. The main restaurant features a towering fireplace in Redwood, the timbered ceiling, the unique recesses, particularly the secluded marble pillared alcove. The exteriors are a joy. The tall slender white tower is a memorial of Elizabeth Gaskell, the Authoress. The famous historic quotations carved into the stonework strengthen the literary and historical aspects. Under the roof of the courtyard is a superb Flemish Lamp. The massive stone columns at the rear of the Courtyard are from St. Peter's Church, St. Peter's Square, Manchester. From the magnificent Italian Roof Garden the views of la belle epoque are wonderful, it is on this balcony that the old cartwheels specially made to carry the massive pillars can be seen.

*Early La Belle Epoque publicity*

contact with and had access to their burgeoning talents, which was what I was seeking. I had little idea, until I met Nick and Sally, how to go about it. I had an idea that Nick Smith had been or was involved in a teaching capacity at the RNCM. I was able to roughly outline to him my plan for bringing classical music to the La Belle Epoque. The Smiths were delighted at the prospect and

71

together we mapped out a programme, with them acting as agents for those brilliant and upcoming musicians.

New musical evenings commenced with a choral concert given by the BBC Singers and then followed, in sequence throughout 1975, the Sartori String Quartet, the Northern Chamber Orchestra, the Festival Brass Consort who played their music on the roof garden, the Alfreton Hall String Quartet and, to end the year, Alan Cuckston delighting everyone on his harpsichord. In the summer of 1976 Chetham's Hospital School of Music Chamber Orchestra played for us, again on the roof garden, as had the Northern Chamber Orchestra. It was then realised that, if we were to expand our activities in a grander musical scene, the sooner the five temporary bedrooms occupying the old concert room came down, the better for us it would be. The classical-music programme ended on what turned out to be a most beautiful piano recital given by Nichola Gebolys, who had won the British National Piano Competition at the age of thirteen, made her first appearance at the Proms when aged seventeen, had broadcast many times and had played piano concertos with leading orchestras all over Europe. Tragically she was to die young and a great talent was lost to the world of music. Sadly, this also brought to an end our association with Nick and Sally Smith and we began our association with popular music and also with jazz, with which I have a particular

affinity and which I love. Meanwhile, Nicholas Smith had become the inspiration behind the formation of the Performing Arts Orchestra for which he was the conductor. This orchestra also included many of the young stars that had played at the La Belle Epoque. It played the country house 'Last Night at the Proms' concerts at such venues as Harewood House, Ragley Hall, Shugborough and Arley Hall, the latter being when I was custodian there. I last saw the Smiths when the orchestra was playing at Erdigg in North Wales. I think it true to say that after so long a time we were pleased to see each other.

It was in the mid-1970s and possibly a year or two after Malcolm's death that I received an offer to buy my share of the business, Dominque, of course, retaining her half share of it. But had she? Or had she assured her brother-in-law, Keith Mooney and his wife Nerys that her share of it would soon be theirs; naturally they were concerned for her and her son. I had not seen much of Dominique since Malcolm's tragic death and I understood her reasons. But it was quite likely that Keith and Nerys had indicated their interest in acquiring her half share. It was no surprise then that the offer to buy did come from Keith and Nerys.

Our first meeting was a strange experience, with Keith being the identical twin of his dead brother – quite disconcerting! I had now, for what seemed an eternity, been starting, acquiring and developing restaurants, taking a gamble or two

A

**MUSICAL AND GASTRONOMIC EVENING**

with the

**SARTORI QUARTET**

at

LA BELLE EPOQUE

60 KING STREET

KNUTSFORD

on

**THURSDAY, 31st OCTOBER, 1974**

at

7-45 p.m. PROMPT — DINNER 9-0 p.m.

TICKETS 6 GNS. INVITATION ONLY          EVENING DRESS

**DINER**

⌖

Charcuterie

⌖

Boeuf Provençal
Légumes de saison

⌖

Salade

⌖

Fromage

⌖

Sorbet au cassis

⌖

Café

*Left: The Sartori Quartet. The Sartori Quartet was actually the first instrumental musical group to play at the La Belle Epoque. However, we were entertained previously by no less than the BBC Singers.  **Right: Le Dîner***

and huge financial risks, most times never seeking or seeing a penny for my endeavours. I had never considered selling my share of the business. Capital gain was not on my agenda. I had given the Tavern to my ex-wife, had not thought of any distant future and was probably naive. I never saw myself as entrepreneurial. Now, here was this offer out of the blue. I was, though, at the time possibly somewhat careworn and a little unhappy with the restaurant way of life and was in fact very tired. I like change and challenge and the La Belle Epoque was by now running beautifully smoothly. The thing that was keeping my interest alive was the prospect of developing the musical side of the business. Initially I was not interested in the offer but after further consideration I accepted. The

A SUMMER EVENING WITH

**THE NORTHERN CHAMBER ORCHESTRA**

ON THE ROOF GARDEN

at

LA BELLE EPOQUE

60 KING STREET  –  KNUTSFORD

on

**FRIDAY, 13th JUNE, 1975**

**BUFFET FROID A LA FRANÇAISE**

Reception 7-45 p.m.　　Music at 8-30 and 11-0 p.m.　　Buffet 9-15 p.m.

Tickets £5-00　　　　　N⁰ 00114　　　　　Dress Formal

---

**THE ALFRETON HALL STRING QUARTET**

at

LA BELLE EPOQUE

60 KING STREET — KNUTSFORD

on

**FRIDAY, 14th NOVEMBER, 1975**

**FRENCH CLASSICAL DINNER**

Reception 7-45　　　Music at 8-15 and 11-0 p.m.　　　Dinner 9-0 p.m.

Tickets 6 Gns.　　　　　N⁰ 00038　　　　　Dress Formal

---

A SUMMER EVENING WITH

**THE FESTIVAL BRASS CONSORT**

ON THE ROOF GARDEN

at

LA BELLE EPOQUE

60 KING STREET  –  KNUTSFORD

on

**FRIDAY, 4th JULY, 1975**

**BUFFET FROID A LA FRANÇAISE**

Reception 7-45 p.m.　　Music at 8-30 and 11-0 p.m.　　Buffet 9-15 p.m.

Tickets £5-00　　　　　N⁰ 00062　　　　　Dress Formal

---

A SUMMER EVENING WITH

**CHETHAMS HOSPITAL SCHOOL OF MUSIC CHAMBER ORCHESTRA**

ON THE ROOF GARDEN

at

LA BELLE EPOQUE

60 KING STREET – KNUTSFORD

on

**FRIDAY, 2nd JULY, 1976**

**BUFFET FROID A LA FRANÇAISE**

Reception 7-45 p.m.　　Music at 8-30 p.m. and 11-0 p.m.　　Buffet 9-15 p.m.

Tickets £7-50　　　　　N⁰ 00064　　　　　Dress Formal

---

*Top Left: The Northern Chamber Orchestra Top Right: The Alfreton Hall string quartet  Bottom Left:The Festival Brass Consort. We were extremely fortunate to be associated with Nick Smith and his lovely wife, Sally. Nick, I believe, taught conducting at the Royal Northern College of Music in Manchester and he guided us in the direction of chamber music groups, of which the Alfreton and Sartori quartets were fine examples of the genre. The other ensembles comprised students from the RNCM, many of whom would go on to become members of various classical music combinations. Bottom Right: Chetham's Hospital School of Music Chamber Orchestra*

La Belle Epoque was still my home, retaining, as I did, a portion of the whole property. I agreed to stay with the Mooneys for a two-year period as part of the deal. It was also agreed that, when I did leave, I would give an undertaking not to open another restaurant within a certain-mile radius. Keith and Nerys were also anxious to develop the musical and gastronomic evening side of the business, which suited me wonderfully well. I was given the rather grand title of Artistic Director; they, however, could call the shots, as it was their money we were investing in the evenings. They had complete confidence in me locating and recommending the artists that were to be engaged. Down came bedrooms and we were off on our new musical adventure. I venture to say that I did not think my new employers would have been too happy with the former classical-music agenda. We had gone down-market. Another huge bonus was, of course, that I was to continue buying the very fine wines and compiling the exclusive wine list.

With the blessing of Keith and Nerys, I was now able to begin a relationship with jazz and the musicians who played it. Since my late teens I had

For the business man, the brasserie offers a unique venue, mid-day luncheons are served "french brasserie style". Here you and your clients are guaranteed quick service and a variety of french dishes and wines.

*The Brasserie menu*

kept abreast of the developing trends and my interest ranged across the whole spectrum, from traditional to modern. A modest record, disc and tape collection reflects my taste. I was now thrilled at the prospect of being able to engage the talented services of some of the best bands and singers in the country, if not in Europe, and, yes, eventually from the USA. At the same time, we had to be cautious and to some extent commercial; not everyone is a jazz lover. Nevertheless, we had a reputation to build and the field was quite open. Not every jazz venue was like the La Belle Epoque; the music has a tradition of being played in seedy, smoky cellars, pubs and the like, which was fine for me and all jazz lovers. Now it was going to be presented in one of the most glamorous and beautiful settings imaginable to an audience who were not necessarily jazz fans and who were largely interested in the classic French food that was being served prior to the music. Where and how, though, to establish contact with these bands? Way back in the 1960s, when on my menswear buying trips to London on behalf of my Harrodian employers and which usually lasted weeks on end, I was glad of the opportunity that presented itself to visit Ronnie Scott's jazz club. It was to them that we now turned as agents acting on behalf of some, if not all, of the bands and singers available.

*Stephane Grappelli. What more can one say about this shy and gentle French jazz violinist that has not been said before? He was in electrifying form and the room momentarily became a Parisian left-bank jazz cellar. Diz Disley and his trio contributed appropriately to the atmosphere*

*A piano recital by Nichola Gebolys. The story of Nichola Gebolys is a tragic one. Having won the British National Piano Competition, aged thirteen, she made her first appearance at the Proms aged seventeen, going on to play concertos with leading orchestras all over Europe, only to die young.*

## BRIEF HISTORIES

### MARIAN MONTGOMERY

We are delighted to welcome back the fabulous American vocalist Miss Marian Montgomery after her tremendously successful appearance at La Belle Epoque last June.

Miss Montgomery enjoys a tremendous reputation for her sophisticated singing technique and her individual and original choice of vocal material. She has appeared in the most exclusive nightspots in America and Europe including The Sands in Las Vegas, The Basin Street in New York, The Talk of the Town in London. Her T.V. appearances have been in the Bob Hope and Johny Carson shows in the States and the Val Doonican, Keith Michel and Mike Parkinson shows in the U.K.

### EARL HINES

Certainly one of the greatest Jazz pianists of all times and recognised as one of the founders of Modern Jazz. Earl studied classical music and started playing professionally in 1922 in Chicago. In 1928 he took part in the famous recordings of the Louis Armstrong Hot Five. Later that year he formed his own famous big orchestra which operated until 1947, featuring in 1942/3 future masters like Charlie Parker and Dizzy Gillespie. From 1948 to 51 he played with Louis Armstrong's All Stars. We are thrilled that Earl Hines visit to La Belle Epoque is the Premier of his 1977 European Tour.

### GEORGE MELLY with John Chilton's Feetwarmers

George Melly is perhaps the first great British Jazz entertainer, the major discovery of the mid 70's although discovery is inappropriate because he created himself in the early 50's when Trad Jazz was really vogue. Outrageous, honest, funny, clever, extremely musical and incredibly diverse, he was voted Britain's number one Jazz singer in a recent Melody Maker poll. A world expert on surrealist art, author of two best selling books, film and TV critic for the Observer and winner of the "Critic of the Year" award.

### "UNDER MILK WOOD" A Jazz suite inspired by Dylan Thomas, composed and performed by the STAN TRACEY QUARTET and narrated by DONALD HOUSTON

Derek Jewell critic to the Sunday Times wrote on 29th February 1976 "I have unsurprisingly always considered Dylan Thomas's 'Under Milk Wood' a minor masterpiece. The Jazz Suite which Stan Tracey wrote ten years ago, inspired by Thomas's work has been likewise hailed. Put the two together though, and you have a transcending experience of triumphant delight, both moving and joyous".

La Belle Epoque has booked "Under Milk Wood" following the huge success of its 1976 tour, and in anticipation of an equally successful 1977 tour.

### SELENA JONES

Glamourous, coloured American vocalist, born in Newport, New Virginia, same birthplace as Ella Fitzgerald. Has appeared in Major Concert Halls all over Britain including the Festival Hall & Talk of the Town.

She has appeared in The Stanley Baxter Two Ronnies, David Frost, Tom Jones, Les Dawson Shows.

## BRIEF HISTORIES

### Humphrey Lyttleton and His Band

Toured Britain with Louis Armstrong and the same year toured with Sydney Bechet. 1959 his band toured America with Cannonball Adderley, George Shearing and Thelonius Monk. During the past 18 years he has moved from The New Orleans Style to the forefront of British Jazz with the emphasis on swing. His all star band includes the Saxophone Stars Kathy Stobart and Bruce Turner.

### The Vintage Syncopators

Are old and trusted friends. They have played their own particular brand of Dixieland Jazz and Comedy in cabaret clubs throughout England, The Continent and North Africa.

### Marian Montgomery

We are delighted to present the fabulous American vocalist Miss Marian Montgomery.

Miss Montgomery enjoys tremendous reputation for her sophisticated singing technique and her individual and original choice of vocal material.

She has appeared in the most exclusive Nightclubs and Concert Halls throughout America and Europe.

She has currently been appearing on T.V. in the late night Mike Parkinson Show. .

### Teddy Wilson

We have pleasure in presenting the legendary American Jazz Pianist Teddy Wilson and his Trio.

In his early days he appeared with Louis Armstrong in Chicago before moving to New York where he joined Benny Carter.

He became an International figure when he and Gene Krupa joined the Benny Goodman Trio.

He was arranger and pianist to the late and great Blues singer Billie Holliday.

### Chethams Hospital School of Music Chamber Orchestra

The buildings of the ancient school date back to before 1420. It became Mr. Humphrey Chethams School 'for the sons of honest industrious and painful parents' in 1656. In 1969 it became a specialist school of music. The Chamber Orchestra is a recent addition to the Schools activities. Its fast growing reputation has led to its first concert to Russia, Poland and Scandinavia which commences immediately after their appearance at La Belle Epoque.

### The Red River Jazz Band

Are a Group of Northern Jazz Musicians playing traditional and main stream music with spirit, drive and with tremendous technical ability. They have played with all the well known British Jazz Musicians

### Larry Adler

La Belle Epoque is pleased to welcome the World famous American Harmonica Virtuoso Mr. Larry Adler. Mr. Adler has made concert and TV appearances all over the world. Recently he has built a reputation on International TV for his wit and humour. He is altogether a remarkable entertainer.

### The Alan Fawkes Modern Jazz Quintet

Alan Fawkes is one of the most highly talented and technically proficient Jazz Musicians in England. His knowledge of his craft and his dedication to it is without question. He is master of his Art on all the Saxophones, Clarinet and Flute. He will appear with a pickup band in October.

### Pepe Martinez

The Seville born Flamenco Guitarist is numbered among the most eminent in Spain apart from his Solo concert appearances on tour in Europe, he has accompanied the most famous singers and dancers in concert, and the customary private gathering of the Spanish nobility. His music and his life in Seville have been the subject of full length television documentaries on B.B.C.2 and Madrid Television.

**The 1977 Musical and Gastronomic Evening programme**

We at first tested the water by hiring a few good local jazz groups before taking the plunge and hiring no less a band than Humphrey Lyttleton's in the February of 1976. He came again on New Year's Eve, famously saying that it was infinitely preferable to play and eat at the La Belle Epoque on New Year's Eve than it was to sit on an upturned Guinness crate eating fish and chips at

Shoreditch Town Hall. Then came George Melly, as wonderfully outrageous as ever. Unbelievably, I had gone to the Band on the Wall club in Manchester to determine the suitability of booking him. It was not that his jazz and his singing would be unsuitable – it was, of course, tremendous – it was to see if his programme was possibly a little too raunchy for a sophisticated Cheshire audience. It was very near the knuckle but we still booked him. We held our breath but his performance went down spectacularly well. It did help that on the front row of the audience were numerous members of the Wilmslow Rugby and Prestbury Cricket clubs, a little raunchy themselves. On the day following the performance, with the band up reasonably early and finishing breakfast, a ravaged-looking Melly appeared on the balcony staircase, clad in silk dressing gown and clutching a cigarette holder. He was then greeted with a shout from the band of "What are you going to have for breakfast, George?". George's throaty reply was "a large gin and tonic, please" – echoes of Noel Coward! Later, and on many occasions, the fabulous American jazz songstress, Marion Montgomery, came

*The grey wine list.* *A further example of the fine artwork provided by Keith Mooney's Colne printing business.*

**HUMPHREY LYTTLETON AND HIS BAND**

at

**LA BELLE EPOQUE**

60 KING STREET — KNUTSFORD

on

**FRIDAY, 20th FEBRUARY, 1976**

**DINER A LA PROVENÇALE**

Reception 7-45 p.m.     Music at 8-15 p.m. and 11-00 p.m.     Dinner 9-00 p.m.

Ticket £8-50                    N 00091                    Dress Informal

**GEORGE MELLY**

with

**JOHN CHILTON'S FEETWARMERS**

at

**LA BELLE EPOQUE**

60 KING STREET — KNUTSFORD

on

**FRIDAY, 1st APRIL, 1977**

Reception 8-00 p.m.     Dinner 9-0 p.m.     George Melly 11-15 p.m.

Tickets £10-50          Nº 00124          Dress Informal

**Humphrey Lyttleton and his band.** *'Humph', enjoying a fine five-course French dinner between sessions, exclaimed "This is much better than sitting on an upturned Guinness crate, eating fish and chips, at Shoreditch Town Hall."*

**George Melly.** *Appearing dramatically for breakfast, clad in a silk dressing gown and brandishing a cigarette holder, when asked what he wanted for breakfast, replied "a large gin and tonic"*

to enchant us all and became much adored by everyone. Sadly, she died in the early 2000s. Britain's leading exponent of the modern jazz piano and composer, Stan Tracey, brought the jazz suite he had composed to the words of Dylan Thomas's poetic masterpiece Under Milkwood, played by his quartet. The poem was narrated by the fine Welsh actor Donald Houston. It was a truly riveting occasion. That gentle, lovable Frenchman, Stephane Grappelli, also delighted everyone with his magically swinging violin, backed up beautifully by the Diz Disley trio.

It was impossible to categorise Larry Adler. The music he played on the harmonica crossed over from jazz to classical music in a twinkle. A great raconteur and humourist, he regaled us with great jokes and wonderful stories. Among the latter was the fact that he used to be asked to play for the notorious New York and Chicago mobster, Al Capone. When Capone felt the need to listen to the then child prodigy, he would ask his most trusted lieutenant to "Get me da kid!" "What kid, boss?" was the question. "Da kid wid da tin sandwich" was the answer. Adler had been living in England for many years, having escaped from the clutches of the witch-hunting anti-communist American senator, Joe McCarthy. Not exactly my idea of a 'red under the bed', Adler had a penchant for the British aristocratic classes and was renowned as being something of a social climber. He was also a lawn-tennis lover and it was my job to try and find him a court or two to play on during his visit, preferably with

**UNDER MILK WOOD**
by
DYLAN THOMAS

performed by
**THE STAN TRACEY QUARTET**
and narrated by
**DONALD HOUSTON**

at

LA BELLE EPOQUE

60 KING STREET – KNUTSFORD
on
**FRIDAY, 6th MAY, 1977**

Reception 7-45 p.m.  Dinner at 9-0 p.m. prompt  Under Milk Wood 11-15 p.m.

Ticket £9-50          № 00107          Dress: Black Tie

**AN EVENING OF WORDS AND MUSIC**

with
**LARRY ADLER**

at

LA BELLE EPOQUE

60 KING STREET – KNUTSFORD
on
**FRIDAY, 3rd SEPTEMBER, 1976**

Reception 7-45 p.m.      Dinner 8-30 p.m.      Concert 11-0 p.m.

Ticket £8-50          № 00086          Dress Formal

*Under Milk Wood. What a magical evening this was! With Dylan Thomas's poem recited by the stalwart Welsh film actor Donald Houston interposed with Stan Tracey's moody interpretation in the modern-jazz idiom*

*Larry Adler, the world-famous harmonica player and raconteur was an escapee from America's communist-hunting Senator Joe McCarthy. Somewhat of a snob, he courted British High Society. Being a tennis enthusiast, a condition of his playing at the La Belle Epoque was that we had to find a private tennis court for him to play on.*

people of a 'superior social standing'. This was not a difficult task, as any number of my old Tavern customers had their own tennis courts. If they could not oblige, one of Toft Cricket Club's wealthy vice-presidents would. By far the most exciting of occasions, and speaking from a jazz-purist point of view, were the visits of the legendary American jazz pianists. Teddy Wilson had been part of the illustrious Benny Goodman trio and quartets in the 1930s and 1940s; he had also been pianist, arranger and conductor of the jazz groups that had backed the renowned jazz songbird Billie Holliday. We also gave a European premiere for Earl 'Fatha' Hines, which was something of an achievement. He considered himself to be the father of the jazz piano, hence the 'fatha' part of his title; doubtless many others, including Jelly Roll Morton, would have disagreed with this presumption.

Nevertheless, Hines in fact had played with the great Louis Armstrong's Hot Five in 1928. I was deliriously happy to be involved; it spoke volumes for their fame that jazz fans from all over England arrived on these occasions, just to stand outside the restaurant doors and windows in an attempt to catch a few snatches of their music. I felt extremely sad that they couldn't come in on those dark winter nights.

By the middle months of 1990 my connection with the La Belle Epoque came to a conclusion with the death in 1989 of my mother, whom I had been caring for in my apartment. It is a particularly sad fact that, in addition to my mother dying, between 1965 and 1989 my father, grandmother and two uncles all died

**AN EVENING WITH**
THE DISTINGUISHED SPANISH FLAMENCO GUITARIST
**PEPE MARTINEZ**
at

**LA BELLE EPOQUE**

60 KING STREET – KNUTSFORD
on
**THURSDAY, 11th NOVEMBER, 1976**

Reception 7-45 p.m.     Dinner 8-45 p.m.     Pepe Martinez 11-0 p.m.

Dinner £7-50          № 00116          Dress Formal

*Pepe Martinez, a delightful and distinguished Spanish Flamenco guitarist, transformed a wet November night into a warm evening in Seville*

within the environs of the Kings Coffee House and the La Belle Epoque. I was then able, as custodian, to engage wholeheartedly in the management and development of business within the walls of historic Arley Hall, seat of Lord Ashbrook and his family. I moved into the hall that same year, 1990, and for six years this role brought much pleasure and satisfaction. Events back in Knutsford were of little interest; I did not become a La Belle Epoque watcher. A return to Knutsford and retirement in 1996, however, took me back home again in 2001 to my terraced cottage in Church View, part of the Lee property which had included the now La Belle Epoque. The cottage was one of eight built in 1886 as a wedding gift from my maternal great-grandfather, Fred Lee, to his then young bride. Remarkably, I was virtually sitting in the lap of the rear of the La Belle Epoque just a dozen metres away. The restaurant had then

been successfully trading for 22 years. Its very nearness bore testimony to its success, if judged only by the volume of music emanating from its rear terrace virtually every weekend. This was never a nuisance.

Being back in Knutsford, however, and so near to what had been my old home and former business, one could hardly escape its affairs. This, after all, was Elizabeth Gaskell's gossipy Cranford and Knutsfordians are relentlessly inquisitive. What did impress them was the obvious success of the Restaurant. Having once been joint owner and manager of the La Belle Epoque, it was comparatively easy to assess such success. No matter, anyway, for the management excelled in self-publicity and its affairs were relentlessly showcased in the local press. It was patently obvious that the La Belle Epoque had been and was still enjoying a golden period in its short history, its glorious interiors creating an atmosphere that had been enjoyed and enhanced by the constant presence of sporting, theatrical and media celebrities. The food, as always, was superb. It had also always been an expensive place to dine, which was of little concern to its wealthy clientele.

Restaurants, however, that have ambition and aspire to such levels of excellence are often beset by problems concerning the preparation and presentation of their food. Much of this emanates from its head chef, who is of necessity an expensive wage item but who also is the key to the success of any fine-dining establishment. It is hard to say that this was the reason that the La Belle Epoque changed its emphasis from quality French cuisine and opted for the highly lucrative wedding reception business, a decision which would prove to be a resounding success. As a wedding venue the La Belle Epoque had had few equals, its glamorous period-interiors again giving it an atmosphere which was quite unique. It was very soon in high demand. No need, then, for an executive chef but just a proficient head-cook and a team that could produce good food in quantity, more about culinary logistics. It was reliably said that the La Belle Epoque held one hundred weddings and other private events in one whole year. Dependent on their size, weddings are expensive affairs and of variable cost. It is well known that this can be over and well above £10,000. The La Belle Epoque can accommodate up to 100 guests. It is patently obvious that turnover could be huge and, with a competent clerical staff, easily cost controlled.

Whatever, then, went so badly wrong? Brought into the very public domain was the news that an ongoing dispute, lasting several years, regarding non-payment by the La Belle Epoque of rent to the Knutsford Town Council, had finally been resolved but not, however, before expensive legal actions had been brought. The situation was determined when the La Belle Epoque entered into a company voluntary agreement (CVA), possibly not giving it due attention and unaware that the CVA legally triggered an automatic forfeiture of the lease. The Council took advantage of this and terminated it. Three months later the La Belle Epoque collapsed as a company with debts amounting to three quarters of a million pounds. Sadly, the La Belle Epoque no longer exists. Presently it is known only by its old postal address of 60 King Street and is awaiting rescue and another identity. One hopes that the next incumbent will be more sympathetic to the old building.

I cannot help but constantly reflect on the demise of a building that meant so much to me and my family. Standing as it does in the centre of town, it is a constant reminder that the building that was opened in 1909 as the Kings Coffee House and that had continued to host the public from 1973 to 2019 as the La Belle Epoque should now after 110 glorious years stand empty, vengefully vandalised as a result of the eviction of the La Belle Epoque for the reasons given. Under such circumstances how can one not feel anything but extremely angry?

This is not the way to end a story but, unfortunately, it is presently the case. One day a clearer picture will emerge as to why the La Belle Epoque collapsed in such a catastrophic and self-destructive manner. However, I refuse to end it in such a dismal fashion. The glamorous old lady that she is awaits her fate. She knows that with care and creativity she has the potential to succeed and magnificently at that. The Knutsford

Town Council presently has plans that appear both ambitious and sound. I wish them and 60 King Street every success in their efforts and who knows whether, by the time this book has been published, there will be every prospect of the sound of people enjoying themselves again within its walls being loudly heard.

*The Front Entrance to what is now, again, 60 King Street, its last occupants, La Belle Epoque Ltd, having left in 2019. Richard Watt firmly emphasised his choice of 'Kings' for his coffee house by engraving the names of all the kings of England on the foremost corner pillar of the building. Of course, his choice had everything to do with its King Street location. This photograph was taken two years after the former occupants had so abruptly departed. The present aspect is of a very sad old building waiting patiently for someone to breathe new life back into it.*